THE COMPLETE BOOK OF
Hang Gliding

THE COMPLETE BOOK OF
Hang Gliding

D. S. HALACY, JR.

HAWTHORN BOOKS, INC.
Publishers/New York

Contents

1   The Sky-Sailers   *1*

2   The Birth and Decline of Hang Gliding   *6*

3   The Rebirth of True Flight   *23*

4   Rogallo Kites: The Flexible Fliers   *40*

5   The Rigid-Wing Gliders   *54*

6   Building Your Wings   *67*

7   Flying Like a Bird   *82*

8   Hanging Higher   *100*

9   Toward the Human-powered Airplane!   *115*

10   Hang Gliding Comes of Age   *129*

Appendixes   *139*

   U.S. Hang Gliding Association Hang Badge Program   *141*

   Hang Gliding Directory   *145*
      Organizations   *145*
      Publications   *148*
      Manufacturers   *149*
      Dealers and Schools   *155*

   Books About Hang Gliding   *175*

Index   *177*

THE COMPLETE BOOK OF

Hang Gliding

1
The Sky-Sailers

IN AN AGE of jet airplanes and space flight, a strange revolution is taking place in the air. Spurning airplanes, and even conventional sailplanes, thousands of people with flying in their blood are taking to the skies in craft called hang gliders that look like those of the Wright brothers and other pioneer aviators. Fittingly, one of the new hang gliders is named *Icarus*, for the mythical Greek daredevil who soared briefly on man-made wings.

The hang gliding craze, which seems to be an outgrowth of the youthful retreat from a technology of mass production and the conspicuous consumption of energy in powered transportation, sprouted wings about a decade ago. Since the first hang pilots leaped from knolls with homemade wings of bamboo and plastic, or "door-jamb wood" and fabric, aficionados by the thousands have joined the ranks. Clubs have sprung up from California to New England and a number of publications, ranging from modest underground efforts to handsome four-color productions, report on the emancipation from noisy, expensive flying machines.

Dave Kilbourne, flying a Rogallo hang glider, was the first pilot to soar one of these craft for more than an hour. *Photo by W. A. Allen*

The hang glider movement created a culture as identifiable as that of surfing, and probably draws many of its members from that sport. "Hang-ins" are part of this aerial way of life, as are treks to ever remoter and higher jumping-off places. Often these are called Smokey-the-Bear expeditions, since they involve national parks. High-flying hang pilots have soared from Dante's View in Death Valley, El Capitan and Half Dome in Yosemite, Pikes Peak, the Alps, and volcanoes in Hawaii. Some have flown behind cars or motorboats and even gone aloft towed by Piper

Cubs or hot-air balloons. Other adventures range from jumping a ramp with a winged motorcycle to getting hooked during a cliffside flight by a surfcasting fisherman!

To the literature of the bumper sticker has been added a new category that includes such gems as "Go Hang," "Get Hung Up," "Look Down on Your Friends," "Go Fly a Kite," "Move Over, Birds," "Let It All Hang Out," and even an ominous "Did You Ever Eat a Pine Tree?" T-shirts are part of the movement too, repeating the bumper messages or extolling the virtues of such hang gliding pioneers as Otto Lilienthal and John J. Montgomery.

A contestant heads for the landing area during the Third Annual John J. Montgomery Glider Championships near San Diego, California, in 1973. *Photo by W. A. Allen*

Forsaking seven decades of aeronautical progress, the new breed of fliers has picked up where such pioneers as Lilienthal, Montgomery, Octave Chanute, and the Wrights left off. In fact, the successful *Hang Loose* biplane was based on Chanute designs of about 1900. Even the popular Rogallo wing, designed for NASA to ease spacecraft back to earth, is a space age, plastic version of the ancient kite in which, centuries ago, daredevils attempted flight.

An estimated 45,000 hang gliding enthusiasts make up this aerial armada of young men and women leaping from the handiest hill or cliff, with wings weighing as little as 30 pounds. While most are content to swoop a few feet above modest slopes, the more expert have already set duration marks of more than ten hours of gliding, and flown at the dizzy altitude of 2½ miles above the ground! Skilled hang pilots climb hundreds and even thousands of feet in ridge winds or thermal air currents. At this writing, one hang pilot has climbed more than a mile and flown fifteen miles cross-country. Some veteran pilots of conventional craft claim they hadn't really flown until they tried hang gliding —shifting their weight for control, and feeling the force of the wind on their faces and bodies as no average pilot ever will.

Added to the aesthetic charm of hang gliding is its economic appeal. A high-performance sailplane may cost $25,000 or more —one reason there are relatively few top-flight soaring pilots in the world. But for the price of lessons in a powered aircraft, the beginner can not only learn to fly a Rogallo kite but buy it as well. If the pilot wants to build one from plans, he or she can do so for a fraction of the cost of a ready-made glider. In fact, hang gliders bring the thrill of flight for as little as $20.

There is an element of danger in flying of any kind, and hang gliders—which as yet are not regulated as are other aircraft—are no exception. Safety is an important challenge the exciting new sport faces.

At the Lilienthal Memorial hang gliding contest at Sylmar, California, 300 craft made more than 1200 flights without an injury. Unfortunately, this excellent safety record is not reflected across the nation and in 1974 a dozen fatal hang gliding accidents were reported by midyear.

Karen Rowley, a top female hang pilot, heads for the takeoff spot atop Green Mountain in Golden, Colorado. *Photo by Jim Gailbreath, Chandelle Corp.*

Thousands of air-minded enthusiasts, most of them young, are experiencing the joys of what they call "eco-flight." On the far horizon are dream craft that will make these pioneer kites as outdated as Model T Fords: "supersoarers" that will launch themselves and then fly cross-country a hundred miles and more, and even truly human-powered aircraft pulled aloft by pedal-driven propellers! Indeed, one such craft has already made a flight of three-fourths of a mile. After centuries of dreams and a hundred false starts, human flight is here.

2

The Birth and Decline of Hang Gliding

> It is a long story of legends and dreams, theories and fancies, all suddenly transformed into facts; a tale of the hopes of madmen suddenly recognized as reasonable ambitions.
>
> *Sir Walter Alexander Raleigh*

LONG BEFORE THE automobile or even the steamboat, there were attempts by bold and foolish men to fly like the birds they envied. The classic tale is that of the pioneer Greek aviators, Icarus and Daedalus. Daedalus seems to have been a forerunner of Leonardo da Vinci, both architect and artist, as well as imaginative inventor. Fleeing his native land after murdering Talus (whose skill was beginning to rival his own), Daedalus and his son Icarus came to the island of Crete, ruled by the great Minos. Minos set Daedalus to work building the Labyrinth, a maze to contain the monstrous Minotaur and the sacrificial humans offered up to him. Then, fearful that his architect would give the secrets of the Labyrinth to others, Minos imprisoned Daedalus and young Icarus on the island of Crete.

As humans had for thousands of years, Daedalus and his son envied the flight of birds, wishing they too could fly across the sea that imprisoned them. In the end, Daedalus built two pairs of wings from feathers, fastening them with threads and wax. But the daring young Icarus failed to heed his father's warning

A fifteenth-century woodcut depicts the ill-fated flight of Icarus and Daedalus. Today a successful line of hang gliders bears the name Icarus.

and flew too near the sun, melting the wax that held his wings together. He plunged into the sea and was drowned. Daedalus sorrowfully buried him on the island that now bears the boy's name and ripped apart his own wings in grief. He believed that the gods had avenged Talus by killing Icarus.

England, too, has a myth of ancient human flight, in which the legendary King Bladud attempted a flight over London town on human-made wings. Like Icarus, he died in the attempt. Human nature in prehistoric times was probably much the same as it is today, and the dream of flight must have been as strong then as now. This makes it easy to accept the mythical tales of Icarus and King Bladud, but for verification of attempts at manned flight we must wait until A.D. 1020. In that year the English monk, Oliver of Malmesbury, climbed a tower and leaped into thin air on human-made wings of cloth. Unfortunately, he contacted the earth with a rude jolt when his wings proved too frail. More tragic was the flight of the "Saracen of Constantinople," killed in a similar tower leap during the eleventh century. His wing was a flowing robe, fitted with slats to stiffen it. Man's dreams of flight were not yet matched by his engineering ability.

In spite of these discouraging object lessons, towers continued to be used as jumping-off places for would-be birdmen all over Europe. In 1503 an Italian mathematician named Dante was seriously injured in such an attempt, and four years later an Italian emigrant to England attempted a flight from Stirling Castle but "fell to the ground and brak his banes." England's John Damian also leaped from atop Stirling Castle while attempting an ambitious flight to France. When Damian crashed he blamed the chicken feathers in his wings, since "they had a natural affinity for the ground." He felt he should have used those of eagles instead!

This was the age of Leonardo da Vinci, the real-life counterpart of Daedalus: artist, engineer, inventor, and dreamer of bird flight. Da Vinci designed and built a clever ornithopter, or flapping-wing craft, based on careful anatomical studies of birds and bats. Apparently his one attempt at actually using the contraption to fly came to grief, and he never again tried to soar like a bird, or even wrote about it. Almost incidentally, he invented the parachute and the helicopter; late in life, he made sketches of what seem to be crude gliders. This modest approach was the one humans had to take—they had to learn to glide downhill before they could achieve sustained flight.

For centuries bold but ignorant men had been demonstrating that human flight was impossible. Common sense told most people that this was so even without trying it but the diehards remained unconvinced. Then in 1680 Italy's G. A. Borelli wrote *De Motum Animalium*, in which he "proved" once and for all that human muscle power could not sustain man in the air. This authority in the field of science informed would-be birdmen that their goal was unattainable. But dreams lived on, and the human spirit and frame are tough indeed. In spite of all the hard knocks and the fatalities caused by man-made wings, ambitious aviators continued to fling themselves from likely castles and bridges. Every year or two some brave soul made the news—and sometimes the obituaries as well. In 1757 one John Childs reportedly attempted to fly from a tower in Boston, Massachusetts, the first attempt at human flight in America.

"Balloonomania"

About this time the hot-air balloon emerged unexpectedly in the forefront of air-flight vehicles and human-powered flight took a back seat to this much safer and more practical means of aerial navigation. "Balloonomania" swept the world. These "bags of smoke" temporarily distracted the tower-jumpers from their risky experiments and doubtless saved some lives, although others were lost in the new lighter-than-air craft, especially when flammable gases ignited. But at last man floated through the air as he had long dreamed of doing. Now it was possible to look down from a wicker basket and get a thrilling bird's-eye view of the terrain. When aeronauts grew tired of drifting where the wind willed, they built dirigibles and launched another branch of flight. There were attempts by balloonists to propel

Engraving shows the hot-air balloon invented by the Montgolfier brothers, which made its historic ascent in 1783.

themselves through the air with their hands, with paddles, or with propellers. But in the end mechanical engines took over.

Balloons were first used for military observation by French forces at Maubeuge in 1794. Napoleon dreamed of using balloons to transport invading troops across the Channel to England. Fanciful drawings proposed a similar job for kites: armed soldiers sent aloft on them would make up an aerial strike force!

Sir George Cayley and the First Airplane

For several decades the balloon eclipsed heavier-than-air craft. But always there was a hard core of thinkers and schemers who felt sure that man could fly as the birds did and not merely bob around like soap bubbles in the wind. One of these believers was Sir George Cayley of England. He made the first documented use of the kite as a glider.

The kite is nearly two thousand years old, according to the estimates of some historians. Chinese kite builders and fliers used their craft in pageants, for sports, for religious events, and perhaps even to carry humans into the air. Oddly, the kite did not appear in Europe for some 1500 years, being one of the best-kept secrets of Chinese inventors, who also kept printing and gunpowder from Western eyes. Chinese legend recalls one "madman" who built himself a kite and fitted it with rockets. Climbing aboard his craft, he had a friend touch off the rockets and departed "in a burst of noise and fire, never to be seen again," according to the story. George Cayley was a more cautious kite builder, fortunately for aviation.

Cayley was an unusual person, and even without his aviation work he left his mark in a number of fields. As a nobleman and member of Parliament he was active in government affairs and civic work. He invented the tension wheel (which we know best as the bicycle wheel), a hot-air engine, and the caterpillar tractor. He established the Regent Street Polytechnic School and found time to write poetry. Of more importance here, we are indebted to him for being the first to work out the correct principles of manned flight, to carry out aerodynamic research, and to make the first real airplane. He had done all this by 1804, at the age of 29.

Cayley wrote the following description of what was probably the first flying model airplane:

> A common paper kite containing 154 square inches was fastened to a rod of wood at the hinder end and supported from the fore part from the same rod by a peg, so as to make an angle of 6 degrees with it. This rod proceeded on behind the kite and supported a tail, made of two planes crossing each other at right angles, containing 20 inches each. This tail could be set at any angle with the stick. . . . The centre of gravity was varied by sticking a weight with a sharp point into the stick. . . . If a velocity of 15 feet per second was given to it in an horizontal direction, it would skim for 20 or 30 yards supporting its weight, and if pointed downward at an angle of about 18 degrees, it would proceed uniformly in a right line forever with a velocity of 15 feet per second. . . .

What Cayley had done was to fly a kite without a string, substituting the pull of gravity for the force of the string against the wind. At last humans had started along a path that would one day take them into the air they had so long wanted to master.

Like da Vinci before him, Cayley clung to the idea of flapping-wing flight. This fruitless idea cost him many wasted hours. But he still managed great strides towards actual flight. He designed working hang gliders, inventing loops through which the pilot could put his arms for supporting his glider. He worked out the speed one must run to get such a craft airborne (13 miles an hour) and had this to say about test flights: "It requires a hill at hand, of a smooth surface and rapid descent. In fact, a mound ought to be prepared purposely, say 50 feet in length of slope with 23 feet perpendicular rise, and then curving off to a continued descent of one in four, for some convenient distance."

Some fifty years after his successful 1804 airplane model, Cayley at last made a man-carrying one. Or rather, it was boy-carrying, as Cayley put it. This glider apparently was the first ever to make a successful flight with a human aboard, for in 1849 Cayley wrote: ". . . a boy of about ten years of age was

SIR GEORGE CAYLEY'S GOVERNABLE PARACHUTES.

Fig. 2.

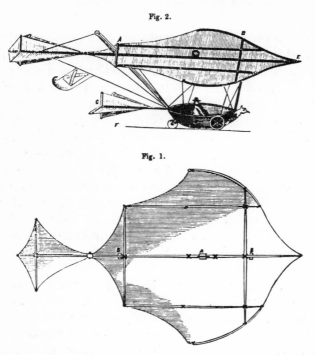

Fig. 1.

Sir George Cayley's governable parachute was probably the first design for a man-carrying glider. *From* Mechanics' Magazine, *1852*

floated off the ground for several yards on descending a hill, and also for about the same space by some persons pulling the apparatus against a very slight breeze by a rope."

Four years later Cayley unveiled a man-carrying craft, which made its historic flight near Brompton Hall, where the inventor lived. Aboard was Cayley's coachman, about 44 years of age. According to eyewitness recollections, this craft "flew across the little valley, about 500 yards at most, and came down with a smash. The coachman struggled up and said, 'Please, Sir George, I wish to give notice, I was hired to drive and not to fly!' "

Ironically, the *Encyclopaedia Britannica* edition published in 1855 considered that Cayley had failed with his flying machine:

"The flying apparatus constructed by Sir George Cayley can scarcely be considered as a successful experiment, since the wings of that ingenious mechanician acted rather on the principle of the parachute, merely floating the experimenter, who started from a moderate elevation, by a very gradual descent towards the earth." The writer had missed the whole point, just as there are still those who miss the whole point of soaring. Cayley deliberately called his craft a parachute, and was well aware that it must glide downward through the air. The basic work was now done, if others could recognize it for what it was. Cayley flew his boy- and man-carrying gliders in 1852, but many years passed before others picked up where he left off.

An American First?

John J. Montgomery was a pioneer glider pilot. As early as 1883 he was building man-carrying gliders; and according to his claims he made successful glides long before anyone else in America. Others say he was unsuccessful until after 1903, when the work of the Wrights again interested him in gliding. At that time he built several new gliders in which he and others made flights from California hillsides. He also used hot-air balloons, which carried the gliders high into the air before releasing them.

According to Montgomery's own accounts, he built for himself, with no help from anyone, a 38-pound tandem wing glider with stabilizing tail surfaces mounted behind the wings. With a younger brother he took this craft to Wheeler Hill on Otay Mesa (south of San Diego) on August 28, 1883, long before the Wrights had even become interested in flying.

The Montgomery glider made the trip to the site in a wagon, covered with loose hay to hide it from the eyes of those who might call young John a crackpot. It is to be regretted that no one did see it and follow the young men to the hill, for according to Montgomery: "There was a little run and a jump, and I found myself launched in the air. I proceeded against the wind, gliding downhill for a distance of 600 feet. In this experience I was able to direct my course at will. . . ."

Montgomery glided down the windward slope of Otay Mesa just as hundreds of other hang pilots have done more recently.

John J. Montgomery shown seated in one of his later gliders. The foot control warped the wings for turns and one hand operated tail controls. *Photo courtesy Rev. A. D. Spearman, S.J., University of Santa Clara, California*

However, great controversy surrounds Montgomery's claims, although later gliders of his did fly, and he himself was killed in 1911 when one crashed. Undaunted, present-day Montgomery fans idolize him. Plans for a replica of his craft have been published and an annual hang glider meet commemorates the historic or legendary Otay Mesa flight of 1883.

Otto Lilienthal: Father of Hang Gliding

There is a modest memorial in Germany, erected in honor of Otto Lilienthal. The man deserves it, and more, for the present hang gliding movement looks to him as father and chief architect. Born in 1848, Lilienthal devoted much of his life to developing heavier-than-air craft. Like other pioneers, he first favored a powered machine of the flapping-wing type. He built models and even full-size craft until the Franco-Prussian War interrupted his work. Later, when his civil-engineering practice would allow, he worked at perfecting a gliding craft to which he could later add an engine.

Otto Lilienthal, shown flying his wood-and-fabric craft down a gentle slope, is generally credited with pioneering practical glider flying. *Photo courtesy The Smithsonian Institution*

Just as his ornithopter's flapping wings had been inspired by birds, his new gliding attempts looked to the birds for inspiration and support. In 1889 he published a book called *Bird Flight as the Basis of Aviation.* Two years later he built his first man-carrying glider. This craft had a single wing, curved like that of a bird, with an area of 107 feet.

Lacking motive power to get his craft aloft, Lilienthal at first tried bouncing himself and his gliders into the air on a springboard! This must have led to interesting and painful experiences, for he soon scrapped the springboard and took to launching himself from an artificial hill he had raised in a small town near Berlin. (It was just about the same size hill Cayley had recommended.) He also made flights from natural hills near the town of Stollen.

Lilienthal's gliders included an open framework from which he could hang by his armpits (the origin of the word *hang glider*) and a vertical fin for directional stability. To maneuver up and down he shifted his weight in the manner so familiar to today's hang pilots. Otto Lilienthal was no youngster but a

Otto Lilienthal's glider not only flew like birds, they also folded up for easy carrying. *Photo courtesy The Smithsonian Institution*

mature gentleman in his midforties. Yet to properly control his birdlike gliders he often had to go through the contortions of a frenzied acrobat. A left turn was made by extending his body far to the left. Swinging the body forward brought the nose down, kicking back pulled the nose up for a landing.

Just as today's hang pilots do, Lilienthal carried his glider to the site in knocked-down condition, assembled it on the spot, and began flying. The day's flights finished, he folded the craft up and carried it home over his shoulder. Lilienthal succeeded in gliding several hundred feet many times, and finally made flights of 1,000 feet, at times 50 feet in the air. However, on August 9, 1896, while flying a glider he had constructed the year before, Lilienthal encountered a severe wind gust, which violently stalled his craft. He immediately swung his weight forward to regain control but the glider turned and plunged abruptly down, to crash from an altitude estimated at more than 45 feet. Otto's spine was broken, and he died the following day in a hospital. His last words were "Sacrifices must be made. . . ."

There were others ready to make such sacrifices to advance the art and science of flying. England's Percy Pilcher was next. His country had a long history of manned-flight attempts, for although Cayley's work had not attracted the serious following it deserved, some had carried on the work.

Percy Pilcher and His Hawk

Pilcher served a few years in the Royal Navy, then resigned to take up architecture and engineering. He became interested in flight and in 1895 built the *Bat*, a glider with about 150 square feet of wing area. Wisely, he visited Lilienthal in Germany to learn more about this new science and during his second visit he flew one of Lilienthal's gliders. Then Pilcher went home and rebuilt the *Bat*, with a horizontal tail for added stability. He succeeded in making many successful flights in it that year.

He went ahead enthusiastically with a second glider named the *Beetle*, and in 1896 he built the *Gull*, which had twice the wing area of his earlier designs. This proved to be too large for convenient handling, and he built the smaller *Hawk*. With 180 square feet of wing area, properly curved airfoil, horizontal and vertical tail surfaces, and even a pair of landing wheels, the *Hawk* was far superior to his earlier designs. Pilcher flew many times in the *Hawk*, and one remarkable flight, in a light breeze, carried him across a valley some 250 yards wide.

Powered flight was in the back of Pilcher's mind all the while and in 1897 he began to work on this project. He could not find a light enough engine so he designed and built his own, a four-horse-power oil engine that was to drive a propeller installed at the rear of the wing on one of his gliders. The engine was not completed until well into 1899 and Pilcher never had the opportunity to install it in a glider. Had he done so he might have beaten the Wrights in making a powered flight in a heavier-than-air craft.

In 1899 Pilcher added a triplane glider to his fleet and in September took it and the trusty *Hawk* to a field for demonstration flights. Rain soaked both gliders but, yielding to the temptation that has often led inventors astray, Pilcher persisted in flying the *Hawk* in his eagerness to interest others. He hooked the glider to a team of horses, rather than using his customary human towing assistant, and on the first try the towline was broken. Pilcher quickly repaired it and the team was started up again. This time, as the *Hawk* zoomed aloft, a bamboo rod in the glider's tail broke with the strain. Out of control, Pilcher crashed hard onto the wet ground. Two days later he died, at the age of thirty-three. Aviation had lost a major force. But there were others to keep the momentum going.

The Wright Brothers

In America, a man twice Pilcher's age was doing his best to get others into the air, since he himself was too old to fly like a bird. Octave Chanute had become interested in gliders when he visited Europe. Encouraged by Lilienthal, he had built several man-carrying hang gliders of biplane design by 1896. With an engineer friend named Herring at the controls, these carefully designed and very stable craft made hundreds of flights, some of them as long as 350 feet, along the sand dunes of Lake Michigan's south shore. Perhaps Chanute's most important contribution was the advice and encouragement he gave to the Wright brothers. He passed on to them all he had learned and even offered to aid them with money. They declined the money but always credited Chanute for his valuable help and encouragement. The latter was of special importance to two inventors whom friends and neighbors thought a little touched in the head.

Shakespeare spoke for most unbelievers when he had the Duke of Gloucester say, "Why what a peevish fool was that of Crete/ That taught his son the office of a fowl!/ And yet for all his wings, the fool was drowned." And the classic poem "Darius Green and His Flying-Machine" by John Townsend Trowbridge typifies the traditional image of the would-be human bird. Its author seems quite familiar with the processes of building one's own wings:

And in the loft above the shed
Himself he locks, with thimble and thread
And wax and hammer and buckles and screws,
And all such things as geniuses use;—
Two bats for patterns, curious fellows!
A charcoal-pot and a pair of bellows;
An old hoop-skirt or two, as well as
Some wire and several old umbrellas. . .

The result of course is colossal failure, when Darius tests his secret batwings:

So fell Darius. Upon his crown,
In the midst of the barnyard, he came down,
In a wonderful whirl of tangled strings,
Broken braces and broken springs,
Broken tail and broken wings,
Shooting stars and various things!

It was against such a background of disbelief that two bicycle builders began their work in a tiny shop in Dayton, Ohio. Today great revolutions in science are generally achieved only by huge team efforts, usually with the expenditure of millions—or billions—of research dollars. The Wrights, using only their own modest earnings from the bicycle business, succeeded in getting man airborne. But they did it in secrecy lest they be considered mad dreamers or worse. Indeed, even after they *had* flown, no one would believe it! Only in 1908, five years after they had accomplished powered flight, did the Wrights stage a public demonstration of their flying machines.

The Decline of Hang Gliding

The Wright brothers made aviation history with the first powered flight in 1903. Prior to that time, however, they had made more than a thousand gliding flights. Their first experiments included towing up an unmanned glider in 1900. Quickly they learned to fly themselves in the breezy air over the sand dunes of North Carolina's coastline. Their longest flight was 622½ feet.

The Wright brothers' first successes were in gliders. In 1911 Orville soared along the low dunes in North Carolina for an endurance record of nearly ten minutes. *Photo courtesy U.S. Air Force*

Even after their great successes with powered airplanes, the Wrights returned to gliding for sport. In 1910, for example, Orville Wright set an endurance record while slope soaring in North Carolina. This mark of 9 minutes 45 seconds stood until a German broke it in 1921 with a new time of 15 minutes 40 seconds.

In the decades since that blustery winter day at Kitty Hawk, however, it is the airplane that has become a potent factor in our lives—not merely as a pleasant sport but as an economic and military force that has completely changed the world. Indeed, so great was the impact of powered flight that gliding and soaring were for the most part long forgotten. Only when Germany was beaten in World War I (the first conflict to use heavier-than-air craft) and barred from building and flying airplanes did gliders begin to make a comeback. On the slopes of the Rhön Mountains, and particularly at the famous soaring site called the Wasserkuppe, a new generation of young men tasted the thrills of flying like birds—first on the familiar slope winds and later in thermals, or bubbles of rising warm air.

The first fliers on the Wasserkuppe rode beneath primitive hang gliders much like those of Otto Lilienthal. But they quickly developed more sophisticated craft: enclosed fuselages with seats rather than simple frames from which the pilot hung; a control stick and rudder pedals in place of basic body movements to control the craft. Half a century later the sailplane is very far removed from the simple earlier gliders in performance—and in price! It is the latter difference that keeps soaring from being enjoyed by more would-be fliers. For a sleek fiberglass high-performance sailplane (which can soar as far as 50 miles for each mile of altitude lost, travel at more than 150 miles an hour, and average better than 90 miles an hour around a 300-mile course) costs from $15,000 to $25,000.

A Schweizer 2–33 sailplane soars on a ridge lift. *Courtesy of Arizona Soaring, Inc.*

Soaring is high sport in its own right, with thousands of enthusiasts, despite the high cost of participation. For most of these pilots, the crude and floppy hang gliders of 50 and more years ago are museum curiosities, designs that have had their turn and should be forgotten. But recently some rebels took a calculated giant step backward—a retreat from sleekness and speed, from comfort and sophistication, back toward true bird flight: hang gliding today is enjoyed in the same kind of craft used by Pilcher, Lilienthal, Chanute, and the Wrights.

In the next chapter we look into the remarkable rebirth of the centuries-old dream of personal human flight—of man with wings strapped to his shoulders and the breeze full in his face as he floats lazily above the earth on a hill wind, or on a rising bubble of air warmed by the terrain far below.

3

The Rebirth of True Flight

". . . From the womb of NASA there was born a Son of multi-colors and whose shape was that of a butterfly. His name was called Rogallo. . . ."

Art Payne, "Whisper of the Butterfly"

AVIATION, IN ITS three-quarters of a century since the Wrights' historic flights, has moved fast and far from the pioneer concepts of birdlike soaring flight. Indeed, there has been a tendency to downgrade nature's winged creatures and to boast that humans have far excelled them. By the middle of this century hang gliding was a quaint relic of the almost-forgotten past. And then something very strange happened: a handful of fliers began moving *backward* in aeronautical time and technology. It was a quiet revolution, hardly noticed at first and generally laughed at when it was. But the romantics persevered, and the result is a new breed of pilots—most of them young and agile—flying the oldest kind of flying machine.

The hang glider revolution came slowly for a variety of reasons. World War II was one of the reasons. Understandably, sport flying was sharply curtailed for the duration of that struggle. There was no gasoline for pleasure flying, no time or material for building civilian aircraft, and little interest in such projects because of far more pressing work. Only the most fanatic refused to be completely squelched. One of these "true birdmen" was Volmer Jensen.

Hanging in There

With powered flight prohibited within 150 miles of the coast during wartime, there were a few little bands of "outlaws" who stealthily built and flew their own aircraft, restrictions or not. Volmer Jensen wasn't such an outlaw, for he built and flew hang gliders rather than power planes. This was legal, although viewed with raised eyebrows. We had passed beyond bird flight forty years ago; why would a grown man—an engineer at that— waste precious time retracing the flights of long-dead pioneers? No matter, Volmer built gliders much like the dusty relics to be found only in museums. The world was not yet ready, nor had it the time, for such powerless aircraft. But the idea lived, and it was destined to grow.

The next great leap backward spanned perhaps thousands of years, for other modern gliding pioneers seized on a completely different configuration to get them off the ground—the venerable kite that the Chinese had flown in the long-past ages. Ironically, NASA—the driving force behind the 4000 mph X-15 rocket plane and a host of spacecraft—was a big factor in this sudden shift from wings and a tail to a simple, diamond-shaped kite.

Mr. Rogallo's Kites

A standard brush-off is to tell someone to go fly a kite, the point being that this is about as useless an activity as one can indulge in. Yet it was the kite that brought flying to the masses on a personal, eco-flight basis. Alexander Graham Bell, best known for his invention of the telephone, was a man of many other talents, and one was for aeronautics. He was a partisan of pioneer John Montgomery and was quoted as saying that all subsequent attempts in aviation must begin with the Montgomery machine. Bell spent a great deal of time on kites of complex design and also built a similar airplane that made one manned takeoff from a frozen lake.

Bell's odd kites looked like huge flying honeycombs. One of them was towed aloft in Nova Scotia with Lieutenant Thomas Selfridge as pilot. The weird kite was smashed in landing, although Selfridge was not seriously hurt. (However, the following year he achieved the tragic distinction of being the first fatality in a powered plane when he and Orville Wright crashed in a Wright biplane being tested for the U.S. Army.) The end of Bell's kite aircraft was the end of kite planes for half a century. The next man to consider this windy weather toy as something more useful has a name that in the last decade has become the word most often used in hang gliding. He is Francis M. Rogallo.

Rogallo, an aeronautical engineer with NASA, had always been fascinated by kites. He flew them as a boy and continued his experiments with new designs as a hobby. In the back of his mind was a way to improve on the conventional parachute by using a kite-shaped one that would move forward instead of settling straight down. Such an emergency device could help military fliers who bailed out over hostile country to glide back to safety. In 1951 Rogallo and his wife were granted the first in a series of patents covering what came to be known as the Rogallo wing. U.S. Patent 2,546,078, issued to Gertrude Sugden Rogallo and Francis Melvin Rogallo on March 20, 1951, begins:

> This invention relates to kites and more particularly to a kite having completely flexible surfaces.
>
> It is an object of our invention to provide a kite of simple and economic construction and wherein the use of reinforcing members may be ordinarily eliminated.
>
> It is another object of our invention to provide a kite which will be simple to fly and graceful in flight.
>
> It is a further object of our invention to provide a kite structure which may be easily folded or rolled and requires a minimum of space in storage.
>
> It is still another object of our invention to provide a structure for a kite having improved aerodynamic characteristics.

Thousands of Rogallo fliers enthusiastically agree that the kite does indeed fulfill all these desirable characteristics—although in

This photograph, taken in 1948, shows Francis Rogallo testing, with the help of his daughter, a kite of his new design. *Courtesy F. M. Rogallo*

an entirely different way than the inventors had in mind! But it took quite awhile from the time the patent was issued for all this to happen. According to Francis Rogallo, the government expressed no interest in his kites prior to the patent application and for a decade after that. However, in 1962, NASA surprised the inventors with a check for $35,000, the largest such award ever made by NASA. (The Internal Revenue Service soon sent a bill for $21,000!)

The first Rogallo kite was diamond-shaped and composed of a keel loosely covered with material. Like a parachute, it got its shape not from rigid structure but from the air filling out the "sail." The craft was cheap and simple, and NASA became interested in this floppy piece of cloth or plastic that functioned like a wing. It was also practically foolproof. The Ryan Aeronautical Company soon built a Rogallo airplane, which went darting about the skies, and the future for the inventor and his simple kite looked booming. But fate was to have it otherwise, and none of the promising applications proposed for the new wing proved practical. Yet, the Rogallo lives on, in the thousands, as the most popular and certainly the cheapest hang glider that can be built. This happened because at about the time the Rogallos were receiving their belated award from NASA a dreamer from California was beginning to think about a new kind of hang glider.

The Bamboo Butterfly

Dick Miller, a gentle and poetic soul who also loved flying, found that he cared less and less for the increasingly heavy, expensive sailplanes featured in the magazine *Soaring*, which he edited for some time. Vacationing on Cape Cod in 1962, Miller felt an old urge to build a hang glider as he hiked along the great sand dunes and thought about the Wright brothers and their experiments at Kitty Hawk. That winter he came across the Rogallo wing idea for the first time and the next summer he built a small model of such a hang glider using dowels and polyethylene plastic. It showed remarkable promise and about a year later he began actual work on a human-sized craft.

Built of bamboo rug rollers and clear plastic, the huge floppy structure was quickly named the *Bamboo Butterfly*. First flight attempts took place in the hills above Hayward, California, and Miller's recollection of them gives some idea of his dedication to hang glider design: "These [attempts] consisted of running headlong down a steep slope in what there then was of the

Richard Miller, photographed in 1966 while test-flying his much-patched *Bamboo Butterfly* at Dockweiler State Beach, California. *Photo by George Uveges*

glider, hastily strapped together for the occasion, and falling into a briar patch at the bottom. . . ."

Miller's bruises healed, while other affairs commanded his attention for about a year and a half, but in November of 1965 he retrieved the *Butterfly* from an uncle's basement and took it down to Santa Monica. He and half a dozen friends, including soaring pilots Lloyd Licher and Paul MacCready, put the Rogallo hang glider together at Playa del Rey beach, not far from the Los Angeles International Airport. There was little or no wind that day, and results were much the same as those he experienced earlier at Hayward, except that there was no briar patch to fall into. According to Miller, MacCready tried a run down the hill using just his arms for lift. He did better than when he used the *Bamboo Butterfly*. So the little band of sandpapered pioneers emptied their shoes, folded up their flying machine, and departed, as spectators jeered.

Undaunted, Miller reconnoitered during the next few weeks and found a better gliding site at Dockweiler State Park. On January 16 the *Butterfly*, now patched with various colors and thus more resembling its namesake, actually flew. Pleased as Miller was, he could not foresee the incredible era of manned flight he had ushered in shortly after the new year in 1966.

The Sky Surfers

Miller admired what he had done, but was willing to improve on it from the standpoint of materials. In his next effort he used a better grade of plastic and metal tubing, rather than bamboo. Called the *Conduit Condor*, this was a more sophisticated flier than its predecessor and made many "buttskimming" flights down the sloping hills above the beach. Miller's crude kites soon triggered a movement that swept Southern California.

Home of many earlier movements, including the great revolution called surfing, the balmy area around Los Angeles apparently harbored hundreds of young men—and a few women—eager to get into the air. The idea's time had come and a new generation of aviators followed Miller down to the beaches around Playa del Rey and to a dozen other sites. They bummed flights from Miller and then began to build their own Rogallos. A little work, a few pieces of bamboo and a roll of cheap plastic and you could get off the ground for long seconds at a time. If a taped joint let go, the fall wasn't far.

In an era of quick and easy copying, sets of plans for hang gliders rolled off printing presses and Xerox machines. Miller's efforts led to the *Bat Glider*, for which hundreds of sets of plans were sold. Another version was called *Batso*, designed by a father-and-son team named Kiceniuk; Taras Senior and Taras Junior. *Batso* used black plastic, of course, and under its huge opaque canopy many fledgling pilots swung and kicked their way from the crest of a hill to its bottom.

A new sport was born overnight. By 1970 hang glider pilots

floated likè gigantic insects over the beach. From shock and out-rage, swimmers' reactions turned to admiration and even envy, as the ranks of hang pilots grew. Here was another form of that Californian sport of surfing. Hang gliding was *sky* surfing, riding waves of air instead of water, with an added dimension that transcended the earlier sport. Rogallo kites became part of the beach scene, and onlookers got used to seeing pilots fling themselves into space, float briefly overhead, land, and scramble back up the hill for another flight.

An early rule of hang gliding urged not flying higher than one cared to fall. This advice proved too tame for many, and accidents occurred. Like skiers, hang pilots came to treat the plaster cast as a badge of daring. Another up-and-down rule was of a more mundane nature: what goes down must be carried up again before the next flight. The exciting glide was paid for only by wearily toting the glider back up to the launch site, and portability became the name of the game. Lilienthal had realized this; some of his designs could be folded up and carried in a bag. Commercial kits began to offer canvas bags, and aluminum tube storage became popular. But there were some new gliders you couldn't put in a bag.

Hang Loose

Jack Lambie, an unusual aviator who has flown not only conventional sailplanes but built and flown replicas of Wright aircraft for the movies, was teaching science to California high schoolers in 1970. Deciding his students needed something that would really involve them, he went back in history to the plans for Octave Chanute's ancient biplane glider. Lambie modified the design into something aptly called *Hang Loose*. Other descriptions included, "A little bit of everything recycled into a biplane!"

Looking more like an airplane than did the Rogallo kites, *Hang Loose* was braced with enough baling wire to encircle the King Ranch in Texas. But it flew Lambie and his ecstatic students. For less than $25, and some hours of hard work, they had produced a real glider that would lift them briefly into the air. The demand for plans to build *Hang Loose* was immediate

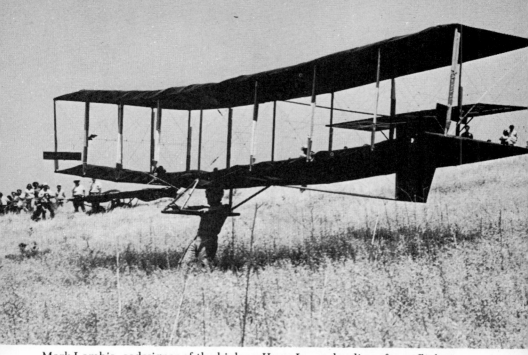

Mark Lambie, codesigner of the biplane *Hang Loose*, landing after a flight in the First Universal Glider Championships in 1971. *Photo by George Uveges*

and tremendous. Lambie and his brother Mark got busy turning out sets of drawings and marketed them for a modest three dollars apiece. As funny as a comic book, they were well worth the price even if you never built *Hang Loose*.

Instead of cutting into a market dominated by Rogallos, *Hang Loose* created even more demand. Many would-be fliers who disdained a kite were turned on by the biplane glider with its authentic antique look. Soon more or less faithful copies of *Hang Loose* were gliding over or smashing gently onto a variety of California hillsides. When they did smash they were easy to repair, often on the spot.

Icarus Lives Again

As Volmer Jensen knew and had pointed out to Rogallo fliers who doubled as acrobats in controlling their craft, the biplane design offered more than a kite. It had a much flatter glide angle, and also lent itself to movable control surfaces. Among

In 1971 Taras Kiceniuk designed and built the *Batso* hang glider, so called because of its black plastic sail. *Photo by George Uveges*

those who appreciated these aerodynamic benefits were Taras Kiceniuk, Jr. and Taras Kiceniuk, Sr. The elder hang glider fan was an administrator at Mt. Palomar Observatory, and a former instructor at Caltech. Young Taras was putting himself through the same institution, working towards an engineering degree with proceeds from *Batso* plans, the Rogallo he developed from Miller's *Bamboo Butterfly*. Both men saw greater promise in the rigid-wing hang glider and they got to work on their own version. Soon the inevitable *Icarus* was flying among the gaggles of hang gliders.

Icarus I was a radical departure, not only from *Batso* but also from *Hang Loose*. A tailless biplane, with wings swept well back, the new craft had wingtip rudders steerable from the "cockpit." *Icarus* flew well, although it was not stable enough to prevent one crash landing.

By late 1971 Taras Kiceniuk had designed his remarkable *Icarus* biplane and was beginning to set new records for performance and endurance. *Photo by George Uveges*

Icarus II used more sweepback in the wing, was slightly heavier than its forerunner, and flew far better than anything then in the air. In October of 1971, flying at Torrance Beach, Taras, Jr., electrified hang glider pilots and spectators. He ushered in a new era by soaring not for a few seconds but for five minutes up and down the beach, making proper away-from-the-slope turns, before settling down for a gentle landing near the surf. Next he moved to the higher challenges of Torrey Pines, farther south. There the cliffs dropped not 60 feet to the sand, but as much as 350 feet, and Taras was soon flying for hours instead of minutes. Sailplane pilots have winch-launched and flown for hours up and down the windswept site since the 1930s. Hang pilots needed no winch, they simply leaped into space with their homemade wings.

Icarus was the first hang glider to be licensed by the Federal Aviation Administration: N55TK, the TK standing for Taras Kiceniuk, of course. The original has been redesigned several times, improving performance with each change. Currently, Taras flies *Icarus V*, a tailless monoplane with much sweepback, still using the familiar tip rudders.

The Skiers Join In

In the 1950s another kiting sport had been born and prospered. Water skiers, having exhausted all the other possibilities of towing behind a boat, dreamed up the exciting idea of going aloft clinging to an oversized kite. Such kites were nowhere near the size or efficiency of present hang gliders, and required great forward speed to go up and stay up. Another variant was towing a parachute in back of a car or boat, with a rider hanging in a harness beneath it. Often this was a commercial operation, offering quick, inexpensive tours of a resort area by parachute tow. Some adventurous people did it the hard way, towing behind a car cross-country, and taking some rough tumbles if they didn't land just right. But it was the ski kites that quickly became popular around the world.

It was inevitable that these daredevils would be attracted to hang gliding with Rogallo kites. Water skier Dave Kilbourne, working independently, built Rogallo kites. At first his kites were

The pilot of this Rogallo kite, which is being towed by a motorboat, will re-lease at about 300 feet and glide down for a landing in the water. *Photo courtesy Cypress Gardens*

towed behind fast speedboats, but Kilbourne looked longingly at Mission Peak at the South end of San Francisco Bay. At length he couldn't stand it any longer and trucked his Rogallo up a back road that zigzagged to the top of the 3500-foot mountain. From there, he launched himself into a brisk sea breeze and flew clear to the bottom of the peak. This first effort was straight into the wind and lasted only four minutes, but in the weeks that followed Kilbourne developed a ridge-soaring technique like that of sailplanes and upped his endurance to thirty minutes, and then to an hour. In the process he acquired the nickname of the "Batman of Mission Peak." On one flight he misjudged and crash-landed in the trees halfway down the slope. Unhurt, and irked at having cut his flight short, he repaired the bent leading edge on the spot (it helps to be a sheet-metal worker), took off and flew back to the top of the peak.

35

Bill Bennett and Bill Moyes, ace "Birdmen" from Australia, also joined the ranks of hang glider pilots, bringing with them the trapeze control bar and the swing seat which eliminated hanging by one's armpits until the circulation stopped. Snow skiers of the more daring variety also picked up the kite idea. Jeff Jobe was a leading exponent, soaring from ski slopes in Utah and Washington state. Like separate streams, these different sports converged and finally coalesced into a unified and massive hang gliding movement.

Eco-flight

A part of the fantastic success of *Jonathan Livingston Seagull* has been attributed to its popularity among Zen Buddhists in the Los Angeles area. It is likely that hang gliding enthusiasts also took the book to their hearts. Author Richard Bach, a poet-mystic sort of pilot, wrote of experiences and values dear to those who seek to fly like the birds. John McMasters of Phoenix calls the entire movement "eco-flight." The introduction to an article by McMasters and Curtis Cole in "Lifestyle!" spells out what they are talking about:

> As long as birds have flown and men have watched them do it, some of us have dreamed of soaring through the air in the same seemingly easy and natural manner. *Not* enclosed in some ponderous metal machine—stuffed with bulkheads and switches and dials and electronic gear—shoved away from the earth by raucous internal combustion engines or screaming jet power plants. Not at all.
>
> What we are talking about is *flying* . . . lifting yourself up on fine, light, feathery wings . . . skimming across the air's invisible currents . . . wheeling and hanging motionless against the sun like some human hawk. Sweet, pure, natural flight . . . buoyed up by the energy of your own muscles, the atmosphere and the sun. *Eco-flight* if you will . . . a whole mind/body/spirit trip.

Surely there was rebellion against the high cost of conventional flying (hundreds of dollars just to learn how), the annoying regulations and restrictions, plus the noise and the

Dave Cronk flies over Torrance Beach, California. *Photo by Carl Boenish*

grime. This was the background that made hang gliding so immediately appealing. It was simple, elemental, clean—and cheap. Miller's *Bamboo Butterfly* cost about $9 to build. Jack Lambie built the more complicated *Hang Loose* for less than $25. Even the commercially produced Rogallo kites could be purchased for several hundred dollars. And this generally included flight instruction as well.

Eco-flight is truly personal flight, relying only on an unpowered craft, a pilot, and the natural environment for flight. Eco-flight craft should be lightweight, portable, and relatively compact. Ideally they should be launched and landed on foot. In the words of Joe Faust, founder of the Self-Soar Association, "Free flight is that flight that uses only foot power, will power, self-power, spirit power, and the free flow of elements of nature. Free flight does not use expensive systems in terms of labor materials or capital outlay. We seek joy, not burden." A dollar of cost and an hour of work per pound of hang glider were set as goals for eco-flight systems costs.

It is easy to comprehend the clean, simple joy of hang gliding and to feel the human challenge of such flight. A sport for reckless, scatterbrained show-offs? Not so. It offers a way of

As pilots gained experience and tired of beach flying, they headed for the back country for longer and more scenic flights. This pilot is going cross-country confronting nature at its exciting best, grappling with the elements for sheer joy and self-satisfaction. For there is little that is practical in hang gliding—as there is little practical in skiing, sailing, or drag racing. Asked how he felt after a pioneering flight from Cone Peak at Big Sur, Rich Kilbourne replied, "I looked out; I just looked around me as I was flying and I could see in all directions and I said, 'This is the finest thing I've ever done.' "

4

Rogallo Kites: The Flexible Fliers

SOARING IS OFTEN compared to sailing. There are differences, of course, since soaring involves the added dimension of altitude. Another difference is that conventional sailplanes have rigid wings rather than the flexible sails used by watercraft. With the coming of hang gliders, however, soaring and sailing moved closer together in this regard, for most of the hang gliders flying today are Rogallo kites. Instead of aircraft wings they more closely resemble diamond-shaped parachutes. (Specially designed parachutes have occasionally been used as hang gliders, with foot launches made from suitable hills.)

A Slow Starter

It is ironic that the early tower jumpers had been so tantalizingly close to the sail idea for so long a time. Many jumped with baggy cloth wings but in general these were built with over-optimistic estimates of lifting ability and thus were far too small. The concept of a parachute that would fall forward was missed for centuries, and this is unfortunate, for the technology was well within the grasp of would-be fliers hundreds of years ago. If Leonardo da Vinci could have seen a Rogallo fly he could easily have duplicated such a craft. He might well have improved it. But ideas seem not to blossom until their time has come.

The closest approach in recent times was that of water skiers who used conventional-shape kites of large size to make towed flights behind—and above—fast boats. It was the husband-and-wife team of Rogallos who, in the late 1940s, provided the vehicle that was to make hang gliding a popular sport. The Rogallo kite was intended primarily as a toy to be flown on a string, but the inventors pointed out ". . . we believe the principle described herein may be applied to man-carrying devices, such as airplanes, parachutes and gliders. . . ." They were quite right, but recognition came slowly and in a roundabout way.

Francis Rogallo receiving the Ed Gardia Memorial Trophy in 1973 for his contributions to hang gliding. Presenting the award is Kas De Lisse, flight director of the U.S. Hang Gliding Association, as Lloyd Licher, president of the association, looks on. *Photo by W. A. Allen*

41

Because of their shape, and the fact that Rogallo hang gliders are generally called kites, it is not well known that they are truly airplanes, and produce lift in the same way more conventional craft do. A kite is flown at a very high angle to the wind, approximately 50 degrees in fact. All its lift comes from the force of the wind under the kite. The Rogallo glider is an entirely different craft. Flying at a much smaller angle to the relative wind, which can be entirely due to the Rogallo's forward motion, the hang glider gets about 70 percent of its lift from the *top* of its wing, just as rigid-wing aircraft do. There is much less strain on the Rogallo wing than on a towed kite, making it safer.

An early experiment used large Rogallo kites for towing heavy military loads. The idea was simply that a larger load can be air-towed than can be carried directly on a tow vehicle. Such loads, ranging from jeeps to heavy containers of supplies, were air-towed over land and water, and in some cases cut loose and allowed to glide—often controlled by radio—to their destina-

This jumbo inflatable Rogallo was tested as a substitute for parachuting space capsules back to earth but was not adopted by NASA as a recovery device. *Photo courtesy NASA*

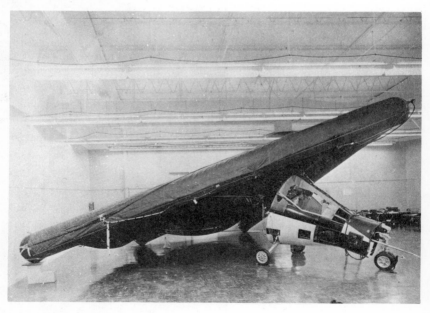

The air force investigated the Rogallo kite as a combination parachute and glider. *Courtesy Ryan Aeronautical Company*

tion. Other experimenters built Rogallo-wing flying boats and land-based aircraft. NASA, for example, experimented with a "Parasev" flying kite. Ryan Aeronautical Corporation built "Flex-Wing" and "Fleep" (Flying Jeep) craft for the U.S. Army. There was much optimistic talk of a revival of the flying automobile, mounting a simple Rogallo wing that could be stored easily in the trunk for ground travel. But such talk tapered off as government funding ended.

The space age had come, and NASA was seeking ways to bring spacecraft, or portions of them, safely back to earth. Millions of dollars were spent in designing, building, and testing Rogallo reentry vehicles for this purpose but apparently NASA found conventional parachutes more suitable. All our astronauts have been safely lowered to ocean recovery sites under huge circular chutes. In the planning stages are stub wings and special lifting bodies, which may serve the spacecraft coming off today's drawing boards. But no Rogallos.

Another application investigated was that of parachuting

fliers from incapacitated aircraft with Rogallo kites rather than conventional parachutes. Such substitutes would be steerable, controllable, and able to carry a passenger three or four miles horizontally for every mile of altitude lost. Thus a bailout at five miles would permit a glide of fifteen or twenty miles, often enough to bring a military pilot safely out of enemy territory, or an overwater flier back to land. However, the Rogallo kite was not adopted for this seemingly useful application either. It was a frustrating situation for the inventors. Here was a beautiful solution but there seemed to be no problems that really fitted it.

Success at Last

Flunking out at higher levels, the Rogallo kite at last found more modest employment closer to earth. By 1974 a special invitational hang gliding contest was held in California commemorating Rogallo's 62nd birthday. He happily attended this affair, even though the weather was so bad that it was termed the First "Fog-Allo" Meet instead. One tribute to the guest of honor described him as the man who gave flight to the masses. And he had done just that.

Because of its utter simplicity, the Rogallo hang glider is surely one of the greatest inventions ever, a unique machine that suddenly and with little warning made the age-old dream of flight for everyone a reality. It is an invention to rank with the sailboat and skis, so simple that everyone thinks of it as soon as they see it—but could not believe it if it were described to them.

Rogallo Aerodynamics

Engineers know a great deal about high-speed flight, and have been able to design and build aircraft that fly at speeds faster than 4,000 miles an hour. As aircraft have become heavier, faster, and more sophisticated, slow-speed flight has been forgotten. A fair amount of bird research has been done, and some basics are known about low-speed flight. But hang glider people have largely had to rediscover these basics and continue the research on their own. Model airplane designers, whose craft also fly at modest speeds, have contributed much.

Mike Markowski's *Skysurfer Kite* shows the basic simplicity of the Rogallo design. The triangular panel at the nose is designed to provide more stability. *Courtesy Man-Flight Systems, Inc.*

Of course, the hang glider is such a simple craft that even without knowing all the facts it is possible to build and fly tolerably good machines. Proceeding on a trial-and-error basis and generally on a very low budget, hang glider design has moved quickly from the primitive forerunners of a decade ago to efficient, commercially available Rogallos.

The sailboat maneuvers on a flat sea and does not move vertically. But a hang glider is free in three axes instead of only two, and adding a dimension greatly increases the possible maneuvers that can be made, or that must be guarded against. It can *turn* right or left, around its vertical axis. It can *pitch* up or down about its horizontal axis and it can *roll* about its longitudinal axis.

The Rogallo, when properly balanced with its center of gravity beneath the center of lift of the sail, will fly in a straight line without turning, stalling, or diving. Disturbed from normal flight, it recovers if sufficient altitude is available. Some pilots demonstrate the "hands-off" capability of their Rogallos hanging from the trapeze bar by their knees and doing other grandstand-

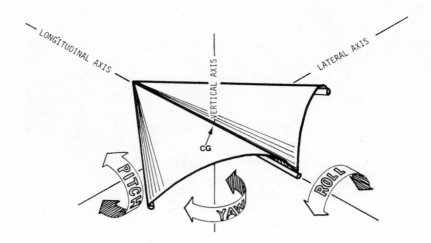

This drawing shows the three axes of a hang glider. *Courtesy Eddie Paul, Whitney Enterprises*

ing stunts. This is definitely not recommended procedure, however. One safety rule says that a hang glider is safe below ten feet and above one hundred—below ten feet a fall probably won't be too damaging, and above 100 feet there is time to recover from a bad position induced by strong gusts or poor flying technique.

The Rogallo sail has no movable surfaces, and control is achieved entirely by the pilot shifting his weight. In early Rogallos this consisted of wildly flinging the legs to one side or the other and sliding the body back and forth. To climb, the pilot shifts the weight aft, thus dropping the tail of the craft. Diving is accomplished by pulling the pilot's weight forward. Moving the body to one side lowers the wing and starts a turn in that direction.

There is no record of any sky surfers having been seriously injured slipping from their lofty perches but there have been some close calls. Certainly hanging in this fashion was wearisome, and that was enough reason to improve on custom. The first refinement was a piece of rope used as a sling to make the flight safer and more comfortable. Then water skiers adopted the plastic swing seat and it became standard equipment on increasing numbers of Rogallos. Water-ski kite fliers also used a "trapeze bar" for control, and the new Rogallos adopted this instead of parallel bars.

Another great improvement was the harness, which permits flying in a seated position or fully prone. Prone flying has two advantages, one obvious and the other appreciated only through experience. Air resistance is greatly reduced, of course, and the prone position also makes hang gliding as close to bird flight as one can get. It offers more intimate contact with nature, just as body surfing excels conventional board surfing in this regard.

The basic metal frame member of a Rogallo is the keel, running fore and aft through the center of the sail. At its front is a nosepiece to which are also attached the two leading edges. A horizontal spreader bar separates the leading edges, and from its junction with the keel the trapeze bar is attached. The seat or harness hangs from the keel. The entire kite is braced with stranded stainless steel guy wires, which give it great strength.

Here are the basic components of a standard conical Rogallo hang glider: A and D—brace wires; B—keel; C—leading edge; E—kingpost; F—noseplate; G—control bar; H—spar; I—sail. *Don Murray, courtesy Eipper-Formance*

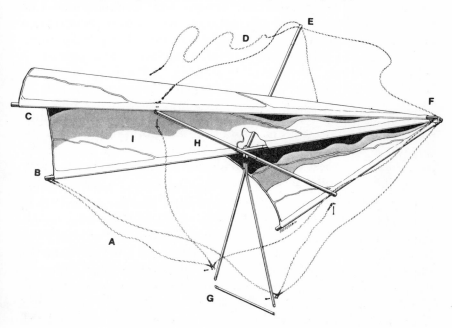

While the Rogallo has rigid aluminum or steel tubing members, its sail uses no ribs to form the lifting surface. Instead the material is limp and assumes the proper shape because of the forces of air it flies through. Rather than being tightly stretched over leading edges and keel the sail is slack and in flight forms two bulging pockets, one on each side of the keel. These give a stubby, gull-winged effect. The Rogallo is still more parachute than wing, however. The sail, of plastic, Dacron, or some other sail material is sewn to fit around the leading edges and the keel, with tape reinforcements where needed. On some kites wooden battens are inserted in the trailing edge of the sail to prevent "luffing" or "slatting" under certain conditions. This is also done on sailboats, although aerodynamicists claim that proper sail design makes such additions unnecessary.

Rogallos range in size from about 15- to 20-foot wingspan. The smaller kites are recommended for pilots weighing about 150 pounds. Such kites are surely the lightest man-carrying aircraft in the world, weighing about 35 pounds. The total weight of pilot and glider is only about one pound for each square foot of wing area. For comparison, conventional sailplanes weigh from about 4 pounds to more than 8 pounds per square foot.

The Good Points

There are great and good reasons for the tremendous popularity of Rogallo hang gliders. From the standpoint of economy the Rogallo is a winner hands down. Simplicity is the reason: the easiest and cheapest way to provide sufficient wing area to carry the weight of a pilot is with the kite configuration. Because the Rogallo is a sail of plastic or cloth, supported by a minimum of light and cheap structural members, its cost is less than a craft requiring a rigid wing, separate tail surfaces, movable controls, and other niceties of design. The Rogallo offers eco-flight in the giant economy size at a price thousands can afford to pay.

Portability is another strong point of the Rogallo. Its inventor has suggested, as a goal of hang gliding, a craft as convenient to carry and to store as a pair of skis. This sounds like a tall order for a man-carrying aircraft, but the goal has almost been

This cylindrical Rogallo is an improved design that gives better performance. Leading edges are curved instead of straight. *Courtesy* The Phoenix Gazette

achieved. It is already possible to carry around a personal glider more easily than a midget sailboat.

An assembled kite is sizable and would require a large garage for storage. Disassembled it stows easily in a handy package. Carried atop a car, or even over the shoulder, the Rogallo is quickly assembled at the site. Subsequent retrieves are easy, and permit many flights in a day, while more complicated gliders must be laboriously knocked down for carrying or manhandled up rough slopes with much help and at a slow pace. Often wheels are seen on Rogallos flown on short slopes; they are not for landing purposes but to make it easier to haul them up the hill.

The great convenience of the Rogallo is appreciated when the day's flying is over. Guy wires are loosened, the crossbar is rotated parallel with the keel, and the leading edges pulled in. The sail itself is neatly rolled around the tubes, the trapeze and seat removed, and the whole package loaded atop the car—or even a bicycle, if that is the only locomotion available. The glider can be carried over the shoulder. Here is the ultimate in sport: climb a likely hill, fly as far as you can, and then pack up and hike to the next site. Some day hardy souls may fly across much of the country in this manner. John McMasters uses the term "flyking" for this sport, noting that the Rogallo also makes a serviceable tent for overnight stops.

A Rogallo kite, once set up, has no moving parts except the pilot. Everything about the sail itself is fixed, and there are no control surfaces, no landing gear, no instruments. Nothing comes between the flier and the sea of air he or she navigates; like a bird the pilot is fully exposed to the elements and like a bird uses only senses and muscles to control the craft. It is true that some designers have added "spoilers" to the tips of experimental Rogallos and "flaps" at the apex, and that basic flight instruments are already insinuating themselves into the pristine simplicity of hang gliding. However, these extraneous additions are not necessary for fun flying.

Except for the skydiver, there is no more direct contact with the elements of flight than in hang gliding. And skydivers, with their outspread arms and stabilizing legs, can only charitably be considered to be flying. Never do they climb, and although they can maneuver remarkably, considering what little they work with, such maneuvers depend on great altitude. Furthermore, skydiving is done at "terminal velocity" speeds of about 120 miles an hour. The key word here is *diving*, and it takes place in a steeply downward direction and only for brief moments.

Called parachutes by their critics, Rogallos are indeed close kin to such safety devices. Parachutes have no trouble with "stalls," the big bugaboo of conventional aircraft. Rogallos will stall, but often the pilots don't realize that they have stalled. The Rogallo is a most forgiving aircraft and tends to merely "mush" downward when it does stall. Because it has directional stability, there is little tendency to turn in a stall, a feature that is not characteristic of many conventional aircraft. Indeed, most aviation fatalities occur as a result of such stalls and the subsequent spins.

In a conventional aircraft, the most dangerous part of a flight is the landing. Even sailplanes sometimes land at 60 miles an hour and faster, sufficient to produce potentially dangerous forces. Hang gliders cruise at about 20 miles an hour (although they can dive faster than that). But they land as slowly as *zero* miles an hour. This they do by adopting the technique of birds, which raise their wings sharply just before touchdown. This exaggerated "flare" greatly increases both lift and drag, and thus the hang glider and its pilot quickly come to a standstill. At most, a few walking steps are needed; at best, the landing is on a spot.

Problem Areas

With all its advantages, the Rogallo has one great shortcoming: its glide cannot by any stretch of the imagination be called flat. In fact, from a height of 100 feet it can glide only 300 to 400 feet in still air. Some rigid-wing hang gliders have a glide angle as good as 10 to 1, making them far better performers. In attempts to improve the Rogallo's performance in this regard, designers have brought the leading edges drastically forward. Some have even straightened them out entirely. The aim is to increase the "aspect ratio," or ratio between the length and width of the wing.

Sailplanes are good performers largely because of their high aspect ratio, sometimes as much as 25 to 1, rather than the approximate 1-to-1 ratio of the standard Rogallo. Experimental Rogallo sails with straightened leading edges have yielded higher than 16-to-1 glide angles in tests, but something has to suffer. In this case it is stability. One manufacturer offers a standard Rogallo for beginners and a short-keel, high-aspect ratio model for "hot pilots only." The Rogallo is a very safe glider in its basic configuration, but making the wings long and narrow reduces stability to the point that the craft is unsafe. Then a set of tail surfaces must be added to restore stability, and one might as well go all the way and make a conventional rigid-wing machine.

To improve performance of the Rogallo, Dave Cronk stretched its wingspan and added control surfaces at the tips. The result was the *Cronk Kite. Photo by W. A. Allen*

Controllability is important in a hang glider, particularly as pilots acquire more skill and want to turn more sharply to fly in ridge lift, or to center themselves in thermals. Relying entirely on weight shifting, the Rogallo tends to be less responsive than some pilots like, and experts occasionally apply a boot to guy wires to bow the keel enough to hurry a turn!

One ironic drawback of the Rogallo is its susceptibility to theft. Stealing a conventional aircraft is a logistics problem, but the portability of Rogallos leads to their frequent disappearance. Indeed, a feature of club newsletters and magazines is a listing of recently purloined hang gliders. However, such action on the part of thieves is a tribute to the appeal of the Rogallo rather than evidence of a shortcoming.

Beyond the Rogallo

All factors considered, the Rogallo is a tremendous machine, and it dominates the hang glider scene so completely in numbers that other types seem rarities. Dozens of manufacturers produce Rogallo wings; surprisingly, no one pays royalties to the man who invented them. However, all hang gliders are not Rogallos. While Taras Kiceniuk was granted an FAA license and number for his *Icarus*, Rogallo builders have been unable to so license their designs. The reason given is that they are not aircraft! Safe, simple, sturdy, and cheap, they are limited in performance. With a sink rate of several hundred feet a minute, they require updrafts of equal strength just to maintain altitude, and very strong lift to climb. Although such lift can be found, and Rogallos sometimes soar for hours, an increasing number of hang pilots are shifting to another kind of glider, the rigid-wing machines like those of Taras Kiceniuk, Bob Lovejoy, and Volmer Jensen. In the next chapter we look at hang gliders far superior in performance to the Rogallos.

5
The Rigid-Wing Gliders

IT IS A TRIBUTE to the many fine qualities of the Rogallo kite that there are relatively few rigid hang gliders flying at the moment, but most serious designers see a bright future for these more conventional craft. This future exists in spite of the relative difficulty in building a rigid glider rather than a kite. It is much easier to build a parachute than an elevator, a rough parallel of the situation we are considering. The parachute is cheaper, lighter, and far more transportable. And although Jack Lambie did produce the rickety *Hang Loose* glider for about $25, it took him and his helpers a long time to get that rigid-wing project off the drawing board and into the air. So there must be advantages to urge designers in the direction of complex, costly, and cumbersome hang gliders.

Performance: The Name of the Game

Performance is the first consideration, and here the rigid glider unquestionably offers far more than its Rogallo cousin. Although Rogallo fliers enjoy the real sensations of flying (and

Early in the hang gliding movement, biplanes threatened to take over. *Photo by George Uveges*

one of them has flown an incredible ten hours and more), the gliding angle of the machines, as we have already noted, is relatively steep. Some say the Rogallo serves well as a training machine, but for real soaring, a craft with far better performance is required. The rigid wing, with a heritage of three-quarters of a century, can and does deliver that performance.

From a small hill the gliding trip in a Rogallo may last but seconds, including take-off run, brief airborne hop, and landing. One hundred feet of height will get you three hundred feet of gliding. To the pilot of a conventional sailplane this resembles a crash dive and he would probably be terror-stricken descending at that angle. Only with strong lift can the Rogallo sustain itself against the pull of gravity. Neither can the Rogallo glide very fast, because of the wind resistance of the flexible sail. But Taras Kiceniuk reports that his latest *Icarus* can fly about 45 miles an hour and still maintain a good glide angle. When he slows to 20 miles an hour his glide increases to 10-1. A hundred feet of altitude thus carries him a thousand feet forward.

A glide of 10-1 is three times that of a Rogallo. And there are other *Icarus* features that make the picture brighter for the hang glider pilot. *Icarus V* has a sink rate about the same as that of a Schweizer 2-33, the trainer sailplane in which most pilots learn. (Or did until hang gliding came along!) Sink rate is a crucial factor when endurance and gain of altitude are the considerations. To remain aloft, a hang glider must be in air that is rising at least as fast as the craft is sinking. In the case of *Icarus V* this is approximately 200 feet a minute. This is weak lift indeed, yet the rigid hang glider will stay up in it while a Rogallo sinks quickly to the ground. It is possible that Rogallos will be able to make cross-country flights under favorable conditions. This assumes that the pilot finds a mountain ridge of the proper length, with wind of the proper speed flowing over it. But the feat is far more likely for pilots flying higher performance rigid-wing machines.

Taras Takes the Lead

It was Taras Kiceniuk who made the first great leap forward—and outward—from the top of coastal cliffs in Southern California. He did this with *Icarus*, his first biplane kite. *Batso*, his Rogallo initial effort, didn't have the kind of performance he wanted, so Taras designed and put together a biplane *tailless* hang glider. Even Lilienthal had seen fit to add tail feathers to his craft for stability, so *Icarus* represented great courage. However, the designers did include wing-tip rudders, controllable from the "cockpit."

Taras started out like many other creative high schoolers; he built a racing sailboat in his workshop at the family home on Palomar Mountain. Then, with a friend, he built a railroad handcar, which the pair frequently lugged over to the nearby Santa Fe railroad tracks for a quick spin along the coast. Named *The Midnight Flyer*, this vehicle got them in trouble with the authorities a time or two but it was great and unusual sport. Then Taras heard about an even more unusual activity called hang gliding, and *The Midnight Flyer* was stashed away in a shed.

Still in high school, he built *Batso* at the age of sixteen, inspired by Richard Miller's *Bamboo Butterfly*. *Batso* was several

Still in running position after takeoff in *Icarus II*, Taras Kiceniuk begins a turn that will take him along the cliffs of Torrey Pines. *Photo by Floyd Clark, Caltech*

cuts above most homebuilt Rogallos, and Taras drew up the plans for it and sold them like hot cakes. The proceeds helped him get started at Caltech, where he was studying for an engineering degree. After that it was hang gliding all the way. Dressed in warm clothes, tennis shoes, and an old-fashioned aviator's helmet with big earphones, the "Birdman of Palomar" was soon a familiar sight, winging his way about the rolling hills near his home. *Icarus* was built of strong aluminum tube spars, ribs of a very efficient curve cut from styrofoam, and plastic wing covering. Fully braced with wire and with parallel bars for hang control, *Icarus* weighed only 55 pounds. The 200-square-foot area of the biplane wings gave the craft a wing loading, with pilot aboard, of well under one pound per square foot.

Icarus promptly outperformed every other hang glider around. Almost as promptly, Taras built *Icarus II*, an even better craft, with a new airfoil, sharply swept-back wings, and generally cleaner lines. *Icarus II* picked up where the original left off and Taras was soon setting endurance records at Torrey

Pines, climbing thousands of feet high in thermal currents. With a speed range from 18-40 miles an hour, *Icarus* had its best glide angle of 8-1 at 25 miles an hour. The sink rate was only 3.5 feet a second.

Taras used an anemometer, or wind-speed indicator, before a flight to make sure the wind was strong enough but not too strong. Setting it aside, he "put on" his glider, poised momentarily atop the steep high cliff, raced a few steps, and was airborne. After that he soared with the big sailplanes up and down the cliffs, to land at last on the beach far below. In flight, Taras lifted his feet to a crossbar up front, thus lowering resistance and being comfortable at the same time. For landing, he dropped his legs, moved back on the parallel bars just before touchdown to stall the big wings, ran a few steps, and that's all there was to it. When a seat became more or less standard equipment, he added that.

Batso plans had sold by the hundreds. *Icarus II* did even better, and a small firm was set up to produce plans, kits, and parts for the glider. But Taras was dreaming up even better craft. *Icarus III* and *Icarus IV* were firmly in his mind. But when *Icarus V* popped into mind, the two earlier designs were shelved, because of his eagerness to build a high performance *monoplane* tailless glider. Completed in 200 man-hours, *Icarus V* has a 32-foot wingspan and an area of 160 square feet. The aluminum-tube, wire-braced wings sweep back sharply, are sturdy enough to withstand a load of six Gs, and are as strong as aerobatic planes. Rudders hang down from the wingtips and work independently for turn control. The craft cannot be stalled and practically flies itself.

Despite *Icarus V*'s higher weight, performance was better than *Icarus II* because of its much cleaner design, which eliminated the drag of wing struts. A swing seat was provided, but Taras still clung to the old parallel bars. The craft had a glide angle of 10 to 1, 25 percent better than *Icarus II*.

At the Fourth Otto Lilienthal Meet in 1974, launching from the 1,500-foot hill at Sylmar, Taras flew for nearly an hour and a half, while the Rogallos were managing flights only a fraction that long. Gliding over the crowd of spectators at about 1500

By flying in a sitting position, Taras Kiceniuk makes his glider more stream-lined. *Icarus V* is the highest performance hang glider aloft today. *Photo courtesy Taras Kiceniuk, Sr.*

feet, he proceeded to circle upward in tight spirals to more than 4000 feet above the ground. He finally came down, landing gracefully, because he was cold. The reception from spectators —and other pilots—was deafening.

With his first *Icarus* gliders, Taras caused enough stir to send hang glider designers back to their drawing boards. A division was shaping up among hang pilots and the leadership of the Rogallos was seriously challenged.

Quicksilver

Dick Eipper, pioneer builder and flier, also turned to rigid-wing design to supplement his commercial line of Rogallos. Designer Bob Lovejoy's first such effort was known as the *High Tailer*, for its prominent rudder design. Next came *Quicksilver*, a more conventional-looking glider than the *Icarus* series, having horizontal and vertical tail surfaces, with a movable rudder for turn control. Wingspan was only 30 feet, with an area of about 120 feet. *Quicksilver* weighed 50 pounds, so with a 175-pound pilot it had a wing-loading of about two pounds per foot of wing area, twice that of the average Rogallo.

Despite its increased weight, *Quicksilver* performed very well, with a glide angle of 8-1, about equal to that of *Icarus II*. In flight it bore a strong resemblance to the old primary glider. Built in the beginning days of conventional soaring, the primary glider had an open-framework body on which the pilot sat beneath the wing. It was launched with rubber shock cord or by towing behind a car. A few are still flying as antiques, but the primary glider is far heavier than today's hang gliders and flies much faster to stay aloft.

Quicksilver was quickly hailed as the craft that would usher in the age of the "wearable monoplane," and the potential of such craft was demonstrated in the flights made by Mark Clarkson of Phoenix, Arizona, early in 1974. A neophyte soaring pilot, with just two hours in conventional sailplanes, Mark switched to Rogallo hang gliders in 1973. From these he progressed to a *Quicksilver* and soon had the hang glider fraternity excited with his amazing flights.

Shaw Butte, a prominence on diminutive North Mountain near Phoenix, rises 800 feet above the clearing used by hang pilots as a landing field. Clarkson soon became a familiar figure with his yellow helmet and rainbow-hued wings. Riding the prevailing west wind and occasional thermals on the Butte, he was soon averaging twice the endurance of the Rogallos. But this was only a prelude. One good day he stepped off the launch site and began circling upward in good thermal lift. When he topped out

Dave Cronk's *Quicksilver*, with its movable rudder, is easier to maneuver than a Rogallo. *Photo by George Uveges*

he was 5,700 feet higher than his takeoff point! The site is also known as Cloud Nine, and that's where Clarkson was by then.

Not wanting to waste such altitudes by merely spiraling back down to a routine landing at Shaw Butte, Clarkson later headed north toward Turf Sailport, site of his earlier flights in 1-26 and 1-34 sailplanes. Shortly thereafter, Turf personnel were shaken to see the diminutive craft jockeying for position in the landing pattern. Clarkson touched down gently on the taxiway for the shortest roll-out of the day!

Clarkson, aeronautically more sophisticated than most of his fellow hang fliers, decided early to equip his *Quicksilver* with instruments that would help him to soar. Thus far, his craft mounts an altimeter and a variometer. The latter instrument is standard equipment in sailplanes, and tells pilots instantly whether they are going up or down. It is almost a must for flights in thermals. Taras Kiceniuk also flies with these instruments, plus an air-speed indicator. Understandably, such instrumentation turns off most Rogallo pilots, who tend to hold out for pilots, wings, and the environment.

Volmer Jensen: Link with the Past

During the World War II ban on powered planes, Volmer Jensen built *So-Lo*, a biplane hang glider with a difference. The pilot clung to parallel bars, but didn't have to rely on acrobatics to control the craft. Instead, hand controls operated rudder, elevator, and ailerons. *So-Lo* has been available for some time in plan or kit form.

In 1971 Jensen attended the first Lilienthal Hang Gliding Meet in Southern California. Watching the steep-gliding Rogallos, he decided improvements were in order and returned home for a huddle with aircraft designer Irv Culver. The result was the Volmer Jensen *Swingwing*. Like *So-Lo*, it had conventional three-axis flight controls mounted in front of the pilot. It was a parallel bar hang glider, but there the similarity ended, for *Swingwing* was a monoplane with no external bracing. A 4-inch diameter aluminum tube formed a boom to carry the rudder and elevator, and a pair of large wheels up front gave the illusion of a conventional craft. The wheels were not for landing, however. They made it easy to pull *Swingwing* back up the slope after landing.

The *Swingwing* had a strange airfoil shape, far deeper than is ordinarily used. This gave great strength to the wing and also a very good glide angle of 9 to 1. The craft flew at 20 to 25 miles an hour and thus was a contender for long flights. The sight of 62-year-old Volmer Jensen floating over the California landscape was proof that you didn't have to be young to fly hang gliders. It also made designers wonder if it wouldn't be well to rearrange the pilot's body to cut down all that wind resistance.

Here is the original *Swingwing*, with Volmer Jensen at the controls. With its high-lift wing and movable controls, this craft performed twice as well as Rogallos but cost far more. *Photo by George Uveges*

Volmer is one of hang gliding's most interesting personalities. He has built a dozen aircraft since 1925, including hang gliders, sailplanes, and two powered aircraft. Among his other designs was the model used for the "Star Trek" spaceship. Surely the oldest hang pilot, Volmer amazed spectators and pilots alike with his two-step takeoffs and landings. Indeed, there was a rumor that he couldn't run more than two steps at his age, until one calm day he proved he could, even while holding the 100-pound *Swingwing*. He wears no helmet, claiming it would prevent him from hearing the rush of wind, necessary for air-speed estimation. Because of his age and his experience with hang gliders, Volmer is often hailed as the missing link between today's hang pilots and the pioneer foot launchers of the old days.

From the start the *Swingwing* proved it could fly when others were sitting it out—and that its control system had opened a new era in hang gliding. But there were detractors as well. "It looks like an *airplane*, and it weighs like an *airplane*," the critics contended. "It just doesn't look like a hang glider!" Also criticized was the trailer necessary to carry it back and forth from sites.

Another old-timer, Waldo Waterman, designed a rigid-wing hang glider much admired at contest sites. Waterman is remembered in aeronautical circles for his "Roadable Airplane," of the 1940s. Now in his eighties, he has turned the clock back with his *Waterman-Seagull Flyer*, a beautiful antique-type hang glider.

Dave Cronk, famous for his *Cronk Kite* and *Cronk Sail*, is a new-generation designer who saw the advantages of the rigid-wing machine. His *Cronk 5* was soon flying with *Icarus* and the Quicksilvers. The pioneering *Hang Loose* gliders have all but vanished from the scene but newer designs have taken their place. Still far outnumbered, the rigid wings are coming on strong, and as formal competition becomes the order of the day they seem assured of greater popularity. Surely the sight of Taras Kiceniuk gently touching down his elegant machine after an impressively long flight, while lesser gliders scratch to stay up for minutes, is strong inducement to fly something better.

The Sailwing: A Blend

The division widens between proponents of Rogallos and those who see rigid wings as the only way to fly but this does not necessarily mean that the two designs shall never meet. Often opposing approaches do meet and merge into an even better synthesis. This could happen with hang gliding, and some preliminary work has been done. The compromise is called the sailwing, a hybrid cross of the Rogallo kite with the rigid-wing hang glider. The result is a conventional wing structure, covered with a loose sail. Instead of conforming to ribs of wood or metal, the sail shapes itself, as it does on the Rogallo kite.

Here, in the eyes of some enthusiasts, is the best of all possible hang gliders: the simplicity, light weight, and safety of a Rogallo sail, plus the aerodynamic efficiency of conventional designs. There have been several attempts in this direction, including Frank Colver's *Sailwing*.

By straightening out the leading edges of a Rogallo, it is possible to create a more conventional wing. The trailing edge might need no bracing or, if it did, wire sewn into the sail might suffice. Somewhere along the line the entire theory of flight changes, for air is no longer flowing through the twin billows formed in the sail but beginning to behave like the air flowing over a bird's wing.

With a long, narrow Rogallo wing we lose stability, and a tail outrigger and control surfaces become necessary. So outwardly the sailwing will look like a conventional monoplane hang glider. Richard Miller has given much thought and encouragement to sailwing design. More help may come from the noted German aerodynamicist Dr. F. X. Wortmann (whose airfoils have made possible fantastic performance in fiberglass sailplanes) who has become greatly interested in the aerodynamics

Frank Colver's Sailwing being readied for flight on a California hillside. Note that this design does use wing ribs. *Photo by George Uveges*

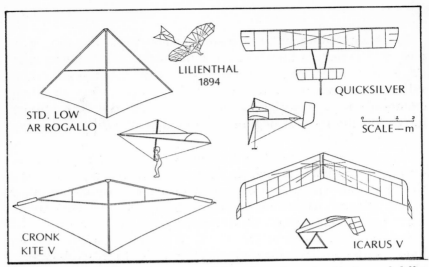

These drawings of a variety of hang gliders show the range in size and difficulty of construction. The Rogallo is obviously the simplest design, but the *Icarus V* is worth its extra cost in terms of performance. *Courtesy John McMasters*

of sails. His findings should benefit Rogallo kites and may in the long run lead to advances in sailwing technique.

A boat sail is an interesting parallel. It generally consists of a sturdy mast, a flexible sail, and lines to position the sail for different requirements. Sails are really wings, which can be aerodynamically designed to better create lift. Although land-lubbers think that sailboats simply catch air in their sails and run downwind, the sail acts much like a wing when moving into the wind. It shapes itself properly in the wind, although rigging, and sometimes battens, are used to prevent luffing or slatting (problems that plague some Rogallos).

No matter how the battle goes—Rogallo, rigid wing, or a sailwing blend of both—hang gliding's future is bright. The thousands already flying are but the vanguard of increasing numbers of people turned on by the idea of personal flight, of launching one's self with a minimum wing strapped to one's back and soaring like a large bird over the terrain below. It is a dream become real—and the price is right. Pay your money and take your choice of wings!

6
Building Your Wings

The cost of the glider, provided the construction is accomplished by the owner, is so low as to place it within the
reach of any person of ordinary means. The expenditure for
raw materials varies greatly. It is usually a little less than
$10 and should not exceed $15.

Popular Mechanics

THE REMARKABLE THING about the above cost estimate for a fly-
able hang glider is that it was made in 1909. It accompanied
plans for a Chanute-type biplane hang glider, still considered
the perfect hang glider by many. Even more remarkable is the
fact that more than 60 years of inflation later, Jack Lambie was
able to build *Hang Loose* for a cost of less than twenty-five
dollars, and that Richard Miller made Rogallo construction
possible for under ten dollars! You are probably going to spend
more money than the pioneers did, but you can still construct a
flying machine that will get you into the air for around a hundred dollars.

There have been three phases in the hang gliding revolution.
The first was its birth, through the efforts of Richard Miller and
his original *Bamboo Butterfly*. Second was the do-it-yourself
phase, with enthusiasts scrounging up materials of one sort or
another to assemble their own wings from available plans. The
third and current phase is that of the commercially available kit
or finished glider. It is a tribute to the varied talents of young

Mike Koman flying his own design—a few lengths of aluminum tubing, some cable, and some plastic sheeting. *Photo by George Uveges*

Americans that a number of the pioneer hang pilots also have had the ability to operate successful businesses in the hang gliding field. Small factories opened in the Southern California area and in other states, including Colorado and Massachusetts. Generally these were small operations, with staff positions filled by the young men who designed the kites and flew them to popularity. Some have grown to sizable operations and have produced hang gliders by the hundreds. The Directory on pages

145–174 gives an idea of the present scope of the hang gliding business.

A great part of the appeal of hang gliding, however, lies in the fact that you can build your own wings. In an age when many are convinced that milk comes from a factory and that food and clothes are synthetically produced, it is refreshing to see people making themselves foam surfboards and homebuilt Rogallo kites. It proves that humans can still *do* things—important and satisfying things—as individuals.

For decades flying enthusiasts have built their own aircraft. The Experimental Aircraft Association has thousands of members, and there are probably thousands of homebuilt powered planes in the air. If you have the opportunity, look at some of these aircraft, which didn't come out of a mass-pro-duction-line in a factory. It will build your confidence, for if another amateur can produce a sleek and slick powered plane, surely you can put together a much simpler hang glider.

In the early days of hang gliding, building such a machine was often a by-guess-and-by-gosh proposition. The average builder simply found some plastic, either clear or black, scrounged up some bamboo poles, baling wire, tape, and rope, and put his Rogallo kite together by main strength and determination. The old phrase "coming in on a wing and a prayer" had special meaning then, and it was fortunate indeed that these homebuilt kites seldom got very high into the air. Today, even more fortu-nately, the guesswork has largely been eliminated, and the process of putting together a hang glider is much simpler and safer.

As hang gliding "went commercial" the wiser manufacturers did some basic research on design, materials, and production methods. Perhaps not all were as diligent as they should have been, but there was a certain amount of policing and regulation on an informal basis within the fraternity. In 1973 hang glider manufacture came of age, and in December of that year the Hang Glider Manufacturer's Association was formed, with 31 firms joining as charter members. Pete Brock, president of Ultralite Products, was elected president of the new HMA, whose goals are safe construction and flight standards. In May of 1974, in conjunction with the Lilienthal Meet, the second meeting of HMA was held. Members devoted most of their time to formulating construction standards for the hang gliding industry.

It is still possible to build a substandard hang glider and to come to grief with it when things go wrong. But this is much less likely now because of the upgrading and standardization of materials. Aircraft-strength parts and supplies are used: nuts and bolts, wire, tubing, and so on. And most hang pilots are so safety conscious that they will spot the flaws in a new glider and quickly and forcefully point them out to its builder.

There are several ways to get into the blue under your own machine. First, if you are a talented do-it-yourselfer you can buy a set of plans for the glider of your choice, get together the materials called for, and assemble the craft. Or you may buy plans plus raw materials from the same supplier. A complete kit is even more convenient, since metal parts are cut and drilled, wires trimmed to length, sail sewn, seat assembled, and so on. The deluxe route to hang gliding is to make out a check for a completed hang glider, which you can assemble, after some practice, in a matter of minutes. This way you can fly at once, instead of trying to figure out how to get part A to fit part B or learning to be a sailmaker with umpteen yards of tricky Dacron or other material. The way you choose will depend on your pocketbook and on the strength of your urge to do things yourself. You can buy a set of plans for as little as three dollars (Jack Lambie's *Hang Loose*) or spend as much as $800 for a completed *Quicksilver B*. Somewhere in that range there is something for you.

Building from Plans

On pages 149 through 174 are lists of suppliers. Hang gliders can cost an appreciable amount of money, so you may want to write first for descriptive brochures. Even better, check out a completed machine of your choice at your local flying site and make sure it lives up to advertising promises and is not too difficult to find parts for and to build. Be very cautious of plans for which no finished hang glider has yet been put together. That neat-loooking drawing may represent the greatest flier of

The builder of this Rogallo set the framework upside down as he assembled the kite. *Photo by George Uveges*

them all—or a pipe dream that won't get off the ground and back down in one piece.

There will be a bill of materials with the plans; pay heed to it. It is not smart to substitute bamboo for aircraft tubing or to use turnbuckles bought on sale at the discount store rather than the type specified. Cheap polyplastic may look like a bargain at your local hardware store, but after you have spent hours taping it to your keel and leading edges you may wish it didn't rip so easily—especially if it rips at an altitude of 50 feet. The same goes for wire, rope, tape, and any other supplies that may be needed. There is now a backlog of ten years' experience in hang gliding construction, so take advantage of it. No need to reinvent the wing.

Thus far the FAA has not required that hang gliders be subjected to the same preliminary testing, regulating, and control required for conventional aircraft. However, the surest way to

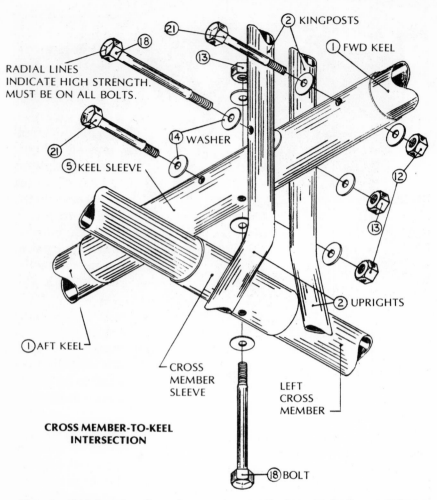

RADIAL LINES
INDICATE HIGH STRENGTH.
MUST BE ON ALL BOLTS.

② KINGPOSTS

① FWD KEEL

⑤ KEEL SLEEVE

⑭ WASHER

② UPRIGHTS

① AFT KEEL

CROSS
MEMBER
SLEEVE

LEFT
CROSS
MEMBER

**CROSS MEMBER-TO-KEEL
INTERSECTION**

⑱ BOLT

This detailed drawing shows how main structural parts of a hang glider are joined. Such work obviously requires some mechanical ability. *Courtesy of Man-Flight Systems, Inc.*

bring this about is to build a sleazy craft that comes apart in the air and lets you down with a bump. Even forgetting all about FAA and its regulations, you should value your own body enough to safeguard it by using approved materials. Whether or not the FAA agrees, you will be flying an *aircraft* and not a toy.

There is an old saying that when all else fails one should read the directions. It is far better to *start* by reading them. Not once, but several times, until you understand them. If you are unsure of your mechanical skills, enlist the help of someone who can read blueprints and who knows how to translate them into an accurate and safe copy of the finished product shown in the drawings and photos.

The Rogallo is a simple machine, a king-size kite put together with sturdy aluminum tubes, stainless steel wire, and sail. If you can read dimensions, drill holes, use a wrench, and tighten turnbuckles, you can probably get the job done. Again, don't let pride stand between you and the admission that you need help. When you are fifty feet above the slope and trouble comes, it will be too late for anybody to help you. There may be a temptation to take shortcuts. For example, you may decide reinforcing bushings in bolt-holes are a bother and who needs them, anyway? Well, you do, if you value your neck. You also need the tape reinforcements called for on the sail.

To build a kite properly, you will need room to spread out. The average garage isn't big enough, for your kite may be a 20-foot square of sail and tubing, leaving you no room to walk around the edges and work. If you have to do this outside, take some precautions for cleanliness. Don't allow the sail to be cut or scratched. Don't let it drag in oil or other chemicals—don't even let it get dirty.

Take time to do the job right. Naturally you are eager to begin leaping from a hill and enjoying the sport, instead of working your head off to make your glider perfect. But the wind will still be blowing next week, and the week after that. Try to get a local expert to check your work as you go along. It's a lot easier to do it right than to do it over. It's cheaper too, for if you drill your tubing or cut your sails inaccurately, it is not wise to patch them up and use them anyhow.

Should you want to build a rigid-wing glider your task will be more difficult and will take much longer. You can look at a Rogallo and then look at *Icarus V* or the Jensen *Swingwing* and see that if you can build a kite in a week, you will be months on the more complicated craft. It will also take more skill. If you have a limited budget you may have to take the do-most-of-it-yourself approach. But be aware that what you are tackling is a more critical project than a sailboat. A life preserver is standard equipment on a boat, but parachutes are not yet available in hang gliders (although the idea has been successfully tried).

If you have built a sailboat, the experience will prove helpful in building your hang glider. So will any mechanical work you've done. And if you're a model-airplane builder you'll find that you're dealing with familiar problems on a larger scale— with the added reward of being able to fly in the finished product. Most model builders have dreamed at one time or another of going aloft in one of their own creations, and hang gliding makes that possible at moderate cost.

Give the designer some credit. You paid him your money so have faith in his product. If parts don't seem to go together the way they should, sit down and study the situation before you get the saw out. Don't be like the careless mechanic who complains: "I cut it off six times and it's *still* too short!"

First the Framework

You have probably figured out that you should assemble the framework first if you are making a Rogallo. This way you will be certain of making a sail that fits on the first try. Note that the sail is a bigger piece of material than would be required just to cover the frame. This permits the sail to billow, making your glider fly better by forming two pockets between the keel and leading edges.

Practically all hang gliders are wire-braced, and the builder must know, or learn about, attaching fittings to the ends of these wires. Special tools are needed, and joints must be tight if the craft is to hold together. Forward bracing wires are also generally coated with a clear plastic to reduce the danger of wire burns should a bad landing throw the pilot forward.

Although the FAA does not ask for rigid design and testing specifications—as yet—some builders may want to check the FAA regulations in F.A.R. 21, the section covering experimental homebuilt aircraft. The Experimental Aircraft Association, Box 229P, Hales Corners, Wisconsin 53130, offers a series of how-to books that hang glider builders with no previous experience may

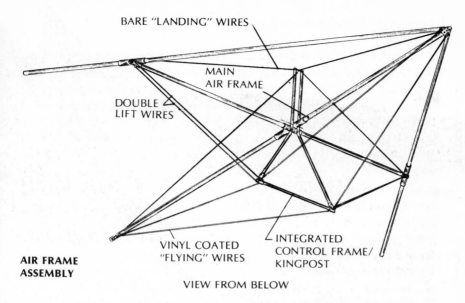

BARE "LANDING" WIRES

MAIN
AIR FRAME

DOUBLE
LIFT WIRES

VINYL COATED
"FLYING" WIRES

INTEGRATED
CONTROL FRAME/
KINGPOST

**AIR FRAME
ASSEMBLY**

VIEW FROM BELOW

This diagram shows a hang glider frame ready for rigging. *Courtesy of Man-Flight Systems, Inc.*

find helpful. Write them for a list. The Soaring Society of America, Box 66071, Los Angeles, California 90066, also publishes a series of handbooks, and the one entitled *Maintenance and Repair* should be of value. It costs only one dollar.

That Little Old Sailmaker

If you are making a plastic sail, some advice is in order. Work on a clean floor, and don't walk all over your polyplastic sheeting with waffle-stompers. Socks are much easier on the sail. Incidentally, if the floor happens to be one with lines every foot or yard or so, you have a built-in measuring device for checking dimensions.

Most plastics are coated with a chemical that must be washed off with detergent soap before tape will stick to the plastic. The tape itself has a tendency to stretch when pulled from the roll, so you should give it time to "relax" to its normal length before applying it. It is embarrassing to have the sail pull loose from the keel or leading edges while in the air, so make sure you use the

Ten-year-old Hall Brock and a friend make Hall's Rogallo ready for flying.
Photo by Dan Halacy

right tape and that you attach it in the proper manner. Since plastic is prone to rip, you may want to crisscross it with strips of fiberglass-reinforced tape. This gives the plastic a rip-stop capacity, so that little tears can't get bigger and let you down. Again, make sure the tape has relaxed before you apply it or you may end up with a much-puckered sail.

The need for neatness applies doubly when you are using Dacron, nylon, or some other sailcloth. First, these materials cost many times as much as cheap plastic. They are well worth the difference, of course, since they are usually rip-stop material and much stronger and more durable than plastic sheeting. You can prolong the life of your sail by not soiling it, scuffing it, or otherwise harming the fibers.

Sewing sails is not for beginners, and even some hang glider manufacturers farm out their sails to professionals—usually people who make boat sails. But the job can be done if you have a good enough sewing machine and use the proper needles and the recommended stitch. Straight stitches tend to pucker the sail, making the seam shorter than the rest of it. So straight seams require a special sewing machine.

Summing up the do-it-yourself approach, it is the cheapest way to own a hang glider and it can be very rewarding. It is also the most demanding method and requires discipline in the way of neatness, workmanship, and following the designer's instructions. When tempted to make a substitution or change, remember that these are your own wings you are building and you don't want them to let you down.

Buying a Kit

If you have the necessary cash or can get time payments on your hang glider, buying a complete kit is a great solution. First, it saves a lot of time, so you can quickly get on with the flying part of your new hobby. Instead of driving all over town seeking parts and materials that local suppliers seem never to have heard of, or buying the wrong quantities, you simply unpack a complete set of materials and parts.

Consult the list of hang glider firms on pages 149–154 to find one that offers the kit you want. Again, ask for a brochure that will describe in words and pictures what you are getting. Some hang gliders are for "hot pilots" only, not for beginners. Should a machine require welding, anodizing, and spray-painting facilities, and your workshop consists of two screwdrivers, one hammer, and a broken hacksaw, you obviously had better look for a simpler project.

Even with a kit there may be construction problems. Again, check with local hang pilots, preferably those with gliders like the one you are building. Examine their finished products and be sure yours is coming along in that direction. Get them over to

Assembling an *Icarus* is more complicated than unfolding a Rogallo. *Photo by Floyd Clark, Caltech*

your workshop or backyard to see if you are doing things right. Don't seek advice from those no more knowledgeable than you. Remember, too, that you can write or call the manufacturer if you get stuck. It's his product that's giving you trouble and he will help you to straighten things out.

Kit building is an intermediate approach to building your hang glider. It will generally cost you more in dollars but may save you enough time and trouble to make up for the extra expense. In some cases you may even find that it costs no more than buying your own materials, since you will not make mistakes and waste money by buying the wrong thing or too much of the right thing. So carefully consider all the factors before deciding on a kit or just a set of plans.

The Ready-Built Hang Glider

The plan or kit approaches are right for two groups of people: Those with limited funds and those who delight in creating something. Many pilots have built the sailplanes that earn them their badges and win contests. Surely there is great pride of accomplishment in flying a craft you have built yourself. But not all of us can do this, and some must settle for buying the finished product. As with the plans or the materials kit, be sure of what you want before you buy. You will be investing far more money, and if the glider proves to be one you don't enjoy—or can't fly—you may have trouble reselling it. There is a market in used hang gliders but depreciation may be high.

Few people buy an automobile just because they like the TV commercials, or the car "looks great." Most prospective buyers want to kick the tires and at least drive the car around the block. The same approach holds for a hang glider. It is easy to say that all Rogallos are alike, and that you might just as well shut your eyes and poke a finger at a list of manufacturers. A far wiser selection method is to find somebody who will let you fly the one you think you want. You may like it. Or you may decide it's a bomb.

In many localities it is possible to buy introductory rides or instruction flights in hang gliders. If you can do this, by all means take advantage of it. Fly not just one glider but as many different ones as you can. Don't rule out the rigid machine because your friend (who just flew four hours in a flexible-wing glider on a practically calm day) says Rogallos are the greatest. By the same token don't decide against the simpler, cheaper Rogallo just because a rigid-wing pilot has said kites glide like heavy rocks. Take every opportunity (and make your own opportunities if you have to) to test a variety of gliders before committing yourself to one particular model. With the investment you are making in it you may have to keep it for some time, and it is far better to have one you will enjoy flying.

Maintenance

Building your hang glider properly is important; so is taking care of it after you have built it and are flying. Because of the nature of the sport, your craft may sometimes be subjected to rough treatment from high winds, landings in rough terrain, and so on. After flying, check it for rips and tears in the sail, or in wing and tail surfaces. Keep wing surfaces repaired and clean.

Check for bent tubes, frayed cables, loose fittings, and other possible trouble spots.

Proper storage between flights is important, too. A Rogallo will be little problem, since it rolls into a convenient package and will fit in an attic, a basement, or a garage. Make sure it will be dry and protected from dust and dirt, harmful chemicals, and excessive heat. A rigid glider will need more space and more care.

Transportation

Transportation is generally a must if you want to fly, so make provisions for doing this safely. Some pilots carry their kites in a rigid tube. Others use a canvas bag. At the very least, the glider should be carefully wrapped so that it will not flap and flutter in

Several hang gliders can be carried simultaneously atop a car or van. *Photo by George Uveges*

the wind or get wet if it rains. A good protective cover also keeps inquisitive hands off your precious machine.

If you are one of the fortunate who lives within walking distance of a hang gliding site, you can put your Rogallo on your shoulder and walk there. Otherwise you must provide some kind of wheeled transport. A bicycle will do in a pinch, especially if you build a rack of some sort to make the job easier. With an automobile the task is very simple, even a Volkswagen serves the purpose. A Rogallo is not much more of a package than skis and poles. And since it *is* so handy, now is the time to learn how to fly this machine you have worked so hard to put together.

7

Flying Like a Bird

. . . Now, there are two ways of learning how to ride a fractious horse; one is to get on him and learn by actual practice how each motion and trick can be best met; the other is to sit on a fence and watch the beast a while and then retire to the house and at leisure figure out the best way of overcoming his jumps and kicks. The latter system is the safest; but the former, on the whole, turns out the larger proportion of good riders. It is very much the same in learning to ride a flying machine; if you are looking for perfect safety, you will do well to sit on a fence and watch the birds; but if you really wish to learn, you must mount a machine and become acquainted with its tricks by actual trial.

Wilbur Wright, 1901

LEARNING TO FLY in a conventional aircraft, equipped with all the instruments and other aids to make the job easier, requires many hours of instruction and costs hundreds of dollars. Personal flight in a hang glider controlled only by body movements is no easy task, so don't get the idea that all you need is a handy hill, strong legs, and lots of courage. Flying like a bird is a difficult and challenging sport that will take time, effort, and ability—which is not to say that it can't be done by most or that it won't be fun. The thousands of hang pilots now flying their lightweight craft—many of whom had never flown before in any kind of machine—can testify to the first fact. You will know yourself how much fun it is the first time your feet leave the ground and you feel—with every muscle and nerve—that you are flying as nearly like a bird as it is possible to do.

This young hang glider pilot demonstrates smooth takeoff technique on a practice hill near Phoenix. *Courtesy* The Arizona Republic

Flying Sites

Equipped with your new hang glider and the determination to fly, you now need a suitable soaring site. If you live in California, Arizona, Michigan, Massachusetts, or near one of the many other established hang gliding sites your task will be easier. If you are a pioneer and there are no active hang glider pilots in your area, you must do some prospecting before you get off the ground.

Hang gliding, sky surfing, or skysailing, whatever you call it, *can* be done in calm weather. In fact, it will be safer if you make your first glides in calm air. But for maximum fun and performance some wind is necessary for you to soar, rather than merely prolong your steep glide. The combination of a suitable hillside and a prevailing moderate wind is ideal, particularly if a road is available for reaching the top of the hill. A hang gliding rule states that you should never fly from a hill you don't want to climb, and one site was labeled "Cardiac Hill" by weary pilots.

Obviously those who live in the flatlands are at a disadvantage, particularly if the area has long periods of calm weather. However, take heart even there. For enthusiasts have sought out Indian mounds, chat dumps (mine waste), and other terrain features that give the needed jump elevation. Some resourceful pilots have launched from multistory motels! If you have a choice, pick a place with rolling hills. These should be as smooth as you can find, for you may stub your toe once or twice and pick up some "road rash" while learning. Arizona hang pilots often end up picking cactus needles from their epidermis, not a pleasant way to end a day of flying.

Many established hang gliding and soaring sites are similar to skiing sites, with slopes of varying difficulty. With experience you will leave the beginner's hill (which flattens remarkably after the first couple of dozen flights you make) and move up. And the day will come when you stand at the top of the big hill, stare at the landing site way down there, and feel much like the circus diver about to plunge from on high into a bathtub full of water.

Preflight

In the excitement to get started with the fun part of hang gliding, don't neglect the very important preflight check of your glider. If something is wrong with it, better to find it out before you get off the ground, not when you are 50 feet up and busy with other matters. Preflighting procedure should never become the hasty business of kicking the nosewheel and counting the wings.

Check first for alignment of keel and leading edges. If you are flying a glider with tail surfaces, sight from the front of your craft to see that they are lined up properly. Check the sail or wing surfaces and tail for rips or other damage. See that all bracing wires and king posts are properly attached and tightened, and that the control bar and seat or harness assembly are secure. (Mark Clarkson learned this the hard way when he fell from his harness while flying at Shaw Butte! Fortunately he was only 10 feet up at the time, and not 5,700 feet.) If your glider has never been flown, try to get an expert to do your preflight check and then to fly it for you. If he can't make it fly, you probably can't either and had better find out what is wrong with it.

Establish a set routine for your preflight check and repeat it exactly each time, so that you won't forget a step along the way. The idea back of these checks is that if you take care of your glider it will do the same for you.

An important part of your preflight check should be the site itself. Make sure the slope is not too steep, and that the wind is blowing almost straight up it. In your excitement to get airborne, don't launch when there are other gliders or spectators in your possible path—and remember that you may glide farther than you expect to. Photographers often get overeager, so guard against running one down. You may smash the camera or, worse yet, your glider.

Good pilot condition also is important. You won't do well if your muscles are so out of tone that it is a great effort to run with a hang glider. Get in shape before trying to learn to fly. As yet there are no physical restrictions for hang pilots, and most people in reasonably healthy condition qualify as potential sky-surfers. However, it is a rigorous sport, so be sure you are up to it. We have noted that what goes down must come back up, and you will find that getting your glider back to the top of the slope requires a lot of physical exertion. Take your time and, if you are winded on reaching the top, take time also to recover, so that you are in good shape for the actual business of flying. It is so demanding that you must be at your best and not gasping for breath when you start your takeoff.

Lighter pilots have the edge over their heavyweight friends. Weight watching takes on special significance in hang gliding, since the lighter the machine-and-pilot combination, the easier it is to stay aloft. Generally, too, the trimmer person is in better physical condition than the overweight type. Take heed, if you need this kind of shaping up—or down.

Some expert hang pilots fly in swim suits and barefooted. For skysurfing along the beach, this may be appropriate for skilled pilots. As a beginner you had better leave such attire to others, however. You may feel something less than birdlike in a sturdy jumpsuit with padded knees, gloves, shoes, and a protective helmet, but it is the safest way to fly. The last item is particularly important. As an advertisement in a hang gliding publication stresses, "Take care of your unique head!" Even beach sand can be very abrasive when you nose-dive into it, and rocky, brushy slopes play havoc with bare legs and arms. As you become more proficient you can ease up on some of the heavy-duty clothing, but stay with the helmet.

Instruction

If you live in a hang gliding area, by all means take advantage of any instruction that is available. Even lectures and movies are a help, and a few lessons supervised by a pro are worth dozens of hard knocks on your own. There are hang gliders rigged with two seats that are big enough for dual instruction. Such training is invaluable, so get some if at all possible.

Proper balance is all-important. Raise your wings too high and it is impossible to get up sufficient speed. Nose down a little too much and you drive yourself into the ground, eating dirt in the process. Remember, even birds must learn to fly, and they are far better equipped for the task than we are. On the other hand, don't let cynics tell you humans weren't intended to fly.

If no formal instruction is available, don't despair. You can watch other pilots and ask for whatever coaching they can provide. In a pinch, you can teach yourself to fly. The fact that Richard Miller, Bruce Carmichael, Barry Palmer, and others taught themselves in far less efficient hang gliders than are now available should be a confidence builder. However, if you are a complete novice, proceed twice as carefully as indicated in the pages ahead. "Low and slow" should be your motto; don't take chances just to impress onlookers. The glory isn't worth the hard knocks.

Learning to pilot a hang glider is easy in a two-seat trainer. *Photo by George Uveges*

The exact details of learning to fly depend, of course, on the kind of glider you are using, your instructor, and the hill, plus you and your temperament. At most hang sites there is a cross-section of types and personalities. Some pilots are ultraconservatives who carefully plot and plan each move, seeming to take forever before they fly from the top of the hill. Others are born birds, or think they are, and fling themselves from the top almost at once.

A ground crew can be a help, particularly during calm weather. Often they assist at wing tips and tail in shoving the pilot from a hill. Or they may pull the hang glider aloft with tow ropes. The main point here is to be sure these helpers know what they are doing. If they are well meaning but not particularly knowledgeable about hang gliders they may hurt you more than they help. Signals must also be worked out and obeyed, so that both wing helpers let go at the same time, for example.

For a time most hang gliding was done in the conventional "hang" mode popularized by Lilienthal. It is not a particularly comfortable position, and it may not be the safest. The swing or seat harness were welcome additions to the hang glider, both for comfort and for controllability. Seats can be used with parallel bar machines or trapeze controls.

The most streamlined and surely the most exciting position for bird flight is prone. Many machines are now fitted with a special harness that permits upright seating, a change to the prone position for flight, and back to upright when it comes time to land. Prone is a chancy way to land; many succeed but one experienced pilot who tried it was killed. Neither is the feet-up, "butt-skimming" landing technique recommended, for this can be very painful and dangerous. The accepted landing position is upright, with the legs in action at touchdown in case some running steps are needed to prevent a three-point landing (two hands and a nose!).

Towing behind cars, boats, or airplanes is far different from self-launching and not within the scope of this book. No attempt will be made to describe those more hazardous techniques, and the reader must seek out professional instruction. While normal stresses on a glider in free flight are only about 50 pounds (the weight of the craft), towing can impose loads of up to 300 pounds, approaching the ultimate strength of the kite. Fatalities have occurred when towing caused structural failure.

The Flying Trapeze

Most hang gliders use the trapeze-bar control system, so let's consider it first. With the nose of the Rogallo on the ground and pointing into the wind, move under the sail and get hooked up in the seat or harness. Rotate the control bar and rest the uprights on your shoulders while you find the neutral position for the sail. This is the point at which there is no pressure on the sail, either up or down. It is important that you quickly get the feel of this position and learn how to maintain it for the takeoff run.

Pushing the bar away from you makes you nose up. Pulling it to you has the opposite effect. Don't think in terms of yanking the bar in one direction or the other but of applying pressure as one does on airplane controls. This is probably a completely different situation than you have ever been faced with, and the learning process takes time. Stick with it, however, and you'll be rewarded.

Up and down control is fairly simple; directional control is more difficult. To turn right, you must shift your weight to the

This hang gliding pilot, using a prone harness, maneuvers his craft by using body English, swinging to the left to start a turn to the left. *Courtesy* The Phoenix Gazette

right by moving out on the trapeze bar and pushing it to the left. A left turn requires the opposite actions. Again, these should be gentle, easy motions and not abrupt ones that will overcontrol and require immediate corrections in the opposite direction. Lateral control requires the instincts and actions of a gymnast in addition to those of a pilot.

Hanging on the Bars

Should you be flying a glider with parallel bars, the launch and landing techniques will be somewhat different. It may even seem easier with a steadier platform than with the rather loose seat-trapeze bar arrangement. Get into the framework, position yourself at the center of gravity, if it is marked, and test for the neutral position. As you find the proper balance points on your parallel bars, you can mark them with tape or use some other form of indicator.

Taras Kiceniuk prepares for a cliff launch in his *Icarus II*, which uses parallel bars instead of a trapeze. *Photo by Floyd Clark, Caltech*

Again in the neutral position, try a few short runs and jumps, barely getting airborne. To nose up you must slide your body aft slightly; to nose down you must slide forward. Lateral control is accomplished by swinging the body right or left. After much practice this becomes instinctive, and you respond to changes in flight attitude without thinking consciously about what you must do.

Getting Airborne

The day may come when we can propel ourselves into the air by pedaling, flapping our arms, or whatever system proves best. Chapter 9 suggests that this day may not be as far off as most people think, but for now we must still seek other means of getting off the ground and into the blue. Some birds have the same problem and must run like crazy, wait for favorable winds, or leap from clifftops even as hang glider pilots do. There are even the kiwi birds, which just never make it. You may suspect a relationship to these unlucky, small-winged creatures at first, but stay with it. The feeling will be replaced by that of a hawk or an eagle as you soar above the beautiful earth.

A conservative way to begin learning is on level ground. This takes more speed and effort, but it is safer. Be sure you face into the wind, and continue to run into the wind. When you think you have sufficient speed, smoothly raise the nose of the kite and get some lift. A major fault of beginning power plane or glider pilots is that of overcontrolling. Nearly all apply too much control at first, and you'll probably do it in your first attempts to get airborne. This will make you stall, slow down, and fall back to earth. Next time try a little less climb. When you do it right you'll make a short gliding jump and smooth contact with the ground on landing.

After a number of level ground hops of this kind you will be ready to try the slope. Don't pick a cliff for this first trial. What is needed is a very gentle slope of about 10 degrees. With your glider comfortably snuggled about you and balanced as well as you know how, you begin feeling things out, testing your wings, your balance, and your ability to make a landing gear of legs that have been used to functioning in contact with the ground.

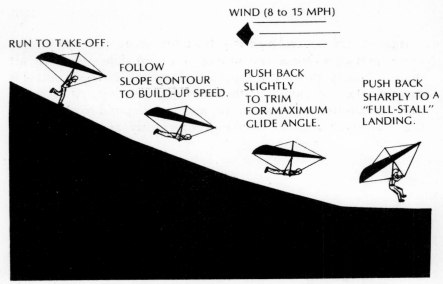

WIND (8 to 15 MPH)

RUN TO TAKE-OFF.

FOLLOW
SLOPE CONTOUR
TO BUILD-UP SPEED.

PUSH BACK
SLIGHTLY
TO TRIM
FOR MAXIMUM
GLIDE ANGLE.

PUSH BACK
SHARPLY TO A
"FULL-STALL"
LANDING.

Here is hang gliding at its simplest. *Courtesy Man-Flight Systems, Inc.*

Now they must get used to leaving it briefly and making contact again, perhaps a bit roughly the first few times.

A calm day is best for this first downhill practice. You will have to move faster to get off the ground, and you won't stay up for long. But the dangers of flipping over backward or nose-diving into the hard slope are minimized. Early airmen used to make very short airborne hops and then let their powered craft settle back to earth. You'll be doing the same thing, gliding only a few feet at a time until you get the hang of it. With practice, the hops get longer, and eventually you leave the hillside briefly and take off like a big ungainly bird for a flight of several seconds duration, with a distance that will match the records of the pioneers!

Your first flights should be straight ahead and not angling to one side of the hill. For this reason, fly with the wind blowing straight up the hill. Otherwise you may find yourself ploughing sideways into the hill with a wing tip. With practice, and a stronger breeze, you can begin making intentional shallow turns right and left as you move downhill. As you improve you will feel less like a captive on a kite and more like the pilot of a glider—or even like a bird instinctively flying through the air.

This glider pilot straightens out for a landing below Shaw Butte, one of the best hang gliding sites in the country. *Courtesy* The Phoenix Gazette

Once having taken off, you are confronted with two more challenges that must be managed properly: the flight itself and the landing. Both are important, and a well-controlled flight obviously leads to a more manageable and comfortable landing. So keep your cool. Shout a rebel yell if necessary, but don't get too frisky the first few glides. Maintain a steady speed and don't let your machine stall. There is no airspeed indicator in front of you and you must depend on the wind in your face, plus the visual appearance of your descent. It will be difficult at first, but do your best and as time goes on flights should smooth out and get easier.

In landing a conventional aircraft, the pilot "flares" just before touchdown to slow the landing. You will do the same, only more so: flaring as a bird does by lifting your glider's nose to a very high angle. This stalls your glider so that your feet touch down with little forward motion. But don't forget in your excitement to get those feet moving, so that you won't nose over on touchdown. And don't stall ten feet up. This is why it pays to use a gentle slope at first and fly only a few feet above the ground as a beginner. Indeed, the cardinal rule for new hang pilots is: Never climb higher than you would care to fall!

Riding the Wind

Your Rogallo kite sinks through the air at a certain fairly fixed rate, probably from 400 to 500 feet a minute. Thus, if you should leap from a suitably sloped hill 500 feet high, you would remain aloft for about one minute on a still day. A minute is an incredibly long time compared with the first few seconds of flight you enjoyed on the shallow slopes. But even a minute becomes short after several dozen flights of this length. And this is where the wind makes hang gliding more interesting, for the wind rushing up a hill cancels out part of the sink of your glider, and maybe all of it. When lift more than matches the sink rate of your machine, a whole new dimension becomes possible: Hang gliding becomes hang soaring, and it is possible to extend the one minute to five, or ten, or an hour.

Currently the hang gliding endurance record is more than ten hours, set along a windy *pali* in Hawaii. Increasingly longer flights will be made, until this category is either outlawed or no longer given much recognition. Endurance marks have not been officially recognized in conventional soaring, since two pilots long ago set a mark of nearly three days—in Hawaii, interestingly. Several soaring casualties were caused by fatigue, particularly with lone pilots attempting new endurance records.

A little wind is good, just the right amount is better, but too much can be a hazard. How much is too much depends on the site, your hang glider, and your flying ability. A twenty-five-mile-an-hour wind is probably too much for safe hang gliding, and gusty wind is worst of all. Wind meters are helpful—wise pilots check the wind before flying. A few pilots attach a wind meter to their craft so that they can monitor the wind speed, and also their own speed in flight. Richard Miller suggests the use of pitch pipes as inexpensive speed indicators.

You needn't even be in the air to be wrecked by the wind! A hang glider, particularly a Rogallo, has a tremendous amount of surface exposed to the wind, and very little weight to hold it down. Improperly handled, it can flip over—and over and over—with the pilot aboard. Never get into the harness or seat unless and until you are ready to fly. It is also advisable to use caution in trying to rescue a windblown kite.

Ridge Soaring

The bold hang pilot soon graduates from hill launching to the more exciting variety known as cliff launching. It is a thrill to run into the air from a slope; it is exhilarating to leap from a high mountain or cliff, such as Torrey Pines, Lake Elsinore, or Shaw Butte. It takes two things: the sure knowledge that your glider will support you, and courage. But every soaring day pilots by the dozens run or step into the sky from awesome launch sites. Often the wind is strong enough that the pilot lifts off the ground with no run at all. In this kind of takeoff, assistance is needed at the nose of the ship to prevent premature lift-off and the possibility of being flung back over the crest by the strong wind.

When conditions are right, cliff launching is the easiest of all, and leads to long soaring flights in wind or thermals, and sometimes in both. The pilot must understand that the wind is rushing over the wing at a steep upward angle, and adjust the glide angle to that wind, and not to the slope itself. Fly relative to the wind, not the ground, or you will stall. So, just after takeoff, you must pull the control bar toward you to get the nose down the proper amount.

Torrey Pines in Southern California has long been the site of conventional soaring. Annual contests have been held for decades, and sleek sailplanes patrolling back and forth in the strong upcurrents along cliffs as high as 350 feet are a common sight. Now more and more hang gliders are joining in, to climb in the wind and do figure eights back and forth with the faster craft. Unfortunately, the number of hang gliders and the carelessness of some of their pilots have created a traffic problem. With good reason, sailplane pilots have objected to this invasion

by the smaller, slower craft. Another soaring site is Lake Elsinore, not far from Torrey Pines. Across the country hang pilots have flown on Cape Cod and along the historic dunes near Kitty Hawk, where the Wright brothers first flew. New sites are being discovered all the time—among them Arizona's Shaw Butte, north of Phoenix and not far from Interstate 17. Rising 800 feet, the sandstone butte provides a long steep hill with a level landing site at its base. Prevailing west winds rush up its slopes on good days, and thermals often abound.

In ridge flying, the pilot makes all turns into the wind and *away* from the hill or cliff to avoid being blown back into the hill. Plenty of altitude is required to make a turn downwind and complete it before landing, so save this sort of maneuver for the day you are able to climb high above the ridge. Too many beginners attempt 360° turns too low and land downwind—often with a crash. Landings should be made into the wind, to take advantage of the lowest possible landing speed. Rarely are landings made back on top of a slope, because of turbulent air currents there. Only when a plateau of some size is used can the pilot safely land on top, some distance back from the edge.

Ridge soaring is of course done on the windward side of a hill, mountain, or cliff. The air that rises over this side curls down on the sheltered, or lee side, and an aircraft caught in this downwash can be forced to the ground. A light hang glider would be especially susceptible to this fate, since it does not have the speed to escape from the sinking air. Wise pilots stay on the windy side of the hill and don't go exploring over the crest. This rule can be bent a little if one has gained a lot of altitude and is high over the hill. Conventional sailplanes sometimes do this to reach the "wave" lift downwind of the hill. Some day hang gliders may fly the wave but at the moment it seems too dangerous.

Thermal Soaring

The world out-and-return distance record for sailplanes is 783 miles and was made in ridge lift along the Allegheny Mountains. However, most soaring is done in thermals, those bubbles or columns of warm, rising air. Hang gliders have begun to exploit

This hang glider pilot soars high above a windswept ridge in Colorado, with snow-covered mountains for a backdrop. *Courtesy of Chandelle Corp.*

An *Icarus II* flies along the cliffs at Torrey Pines, where flights of several hours are possible. *Photo by Floyd Clark, Caltech*

these handy up elevators, often marked at the bottom by dust devils and at the top by puffy cumulus clouds.

Taras Kiceniuk's *Icarus II* was one of the first hang gliders to explore thermal soaring. We have noted that his new *Icarus V* has a sink speed about the same as the Schweizer 2-33, standard trainer for most sailplane pilots. Because *Icarus* has a much slower speed and smaller turning radius, it should be able to climb faster than the 2-33, which is excellent at thermaling.

Good thermals go up about 500 feet a minute, and sometimes 1,000 feet a minute and more is encountered.

The main problem for hang gliders is the violent turbulence sometimes associated with thermal lift. Surely a hang glider flight in a strong thermal is more exciting than it is in a sailplane weighing 500 pounds or more! Hang pilots have described the thrill—and the jolting physical impact—of working a strong thermal.

The Best Is Yet to Come!

Obviously many hang pilots no longer take seriously the warning about climbing no higher than they would care to fall. Neither do any routinely wear parachutes, although the day may come when these are required equipment for high-soaring flights. But the hang glider pilot does not intend to fall. Most sailplane instruction and rental flights are made without parachutes, as is power-plane instruction and pleasure flying. Hang gliders fly slower and are inherently safer, so they tend to let pilots down much easier than heavier craft do.

A short flight in a hang glider, with your feet skimming the ground, is a heady thrill when you are just getting started. But such flights are in another sense just skimming the surface. The next chapter explores the greater joys of hang gliding, a sport that seems bounded only by designer skill, pilot ability, and the challenging sky.

8
Hanging Higher

THE COVER OF *Soaring* magazine for May 1974 featured a color photo of Torrey Pines in Southern California. Soaring above the 350-foot cliffs was one lone sailplane. Darting around it were four Rogallo kites, their pilots nonchalantly flying hundreds of feet above the surf. Unless one has done this sort of thing, the thrill of hang soaring can only be imagined. Instead of being imprisoned in a tight cockpit sealed over with Plexiglas, hang pilots fly free and easy, actually feeling the wind currents on their bodies as well as against the sails of their craft.

The Stunt Flyers

Spectacular as such a sight is, it represents routine flying for many hang pilots. Even the excitement of soaring like a bird palled after so many flights, and daredevil pilots sought new thrills. One of the first was to put the trapeze control bar to its original use—as a trapeze for acrobatics. Soon experts like the Wills brothers were hanging by their knees, arms waving in the breeze as their stable and sturdy craft flew along on their own.

Spot-landing contests offered a challenge too, and the champions began aiming for bull's-eyes, directing their craft like huge blunt darts at circles painted in the landing area. The spot-landing craze spread quickly. USHGA's Hang Gliding Park at Sylmar solved the problem of pilots landing on private property very neatly. Circles were whitewashed in the landing area and from then on hang pilots bent every effort to hit them! Here was more proof of the controllability of the new craft, as well as of the skill of their pilots.

Among the hottest acrobats were the kite skiers, and annual Delta Kite Championships were staged at Cypress Gardens, Florida, home of all sorts of competitive skiing. Events included spot landings, endurance in free flight, and aerobatics. Contestants took advantage of thermals rising from grandstand roofs. To gain maximum altitude from their 500-foot tow ropes, they used faster boats and zoomed sharply up at release for extra tens of feet of altitude before beginning their routines.

Champion Bob Wills scores a bulls-eye in spot landing competiton. His flying attire is not recommended for the average pilot. *Courtesy Sport Kites, Inc.*

Hang pilots have towed high over the San Francisco–Oakland Bay bridge and the Statue of Liberty. In 1967, after only five weeks of flying, Australia's Bill Moyes was the first to exceed 1000 feet on a kite towed from the back of a boat. In 1968 he upped this to 2870 feet and also self-launched on skis from Mt. Crackenback in the Australian Alps and flew to Thredbo Village, a distance of 1½ miles. The same year he was towed behind a boat for 190 miles in 6 hours 55 minutes (he was trying for 500 miles but the boat sank). In 1969 he glided from the rim of the Grand Canyon to Phantom Ranch in 8 minutes 32 seconds. This flight was 4.7 miles long and descended 4,800 feet.

Water-ski kite fliers developed fantastic skills and demonstrated daring to match. Moyes and his countryman Bill Bennett challenged each other with successively higher tows behind speedboats at Lake Havasu in Arizona. Bennett reached 3000 feet in this manner, then Moyes had himself towed to 4000 feet—back of a Piper Super Cub! Not only that, he promptly gained another 750 feet in thermals. Batman Dave Kilbourne outdid them all by hitching a ride beneath a hot-air balloon to 9000 feet over the Sacramento Valley and releasing. This was heady stuff, nearly 2 miles high, hanging from the bar of a Rogallo kite with nothing but air between pilot and terrain.

A variant of hang gliding sprang up on several ski slopes around the country. Jeff Jobe pioneered in making hang gliding a snow sport. A water skier at the age of 15, he was soon taking off under a big kite. Eventually he learned to climb to 900 feet and release, gliding back down to the lake. When he took to snow skiing, he found that the kite worked even better. He startled skiers at Apental, near Seattle, and then moved to Snowbird, Utah. That name was perfect for his specialty. Primarily a ski instructor, he soon was spending his free time flying his Rogallo off the steep slopes. So popular was the sight of a human birdman high above the mountain that he was hired at $500 a day to make exhibition flights.

This water skier, towed aloft behind a boat, is now in free flight, maneuvering toward a spot landing. *Courtesy Cypress Gardens*

A kite gives this ski jumper a lot of extra lift. *Courtesy Delta Wing Kites*

After soaring as high as 3000 feet above the wooded slopes, Jobe would select a level or slightly uphill slope and come in for a smooth landing on his skis. Only once did he have difficulty, landing in the trees. Here was a combination of two of the most exciting sports, with an ease of takeoff unknown on ordinary soaring hills. A kite provides a ski jumper's dream: long soaring flights, with turns as desired, and a smooth landing at the end.

Because much hang gliding is done near water, a few overbold pilots have landed in the briny. For this reason, some have adopted the water-ski kiters' practice of adding floats to the end of their control bars and learned how to get loose quickly from their rigging.

Outfoxing Smokey the Bear

In many ways hang pilots are like mountain climbers. They fly a hill because it's there and then go searching for a higher one. Dante's View in Death Valley was one such height, conquered by the hang glider when Bill Bennett leaped from the 6000-foot height and glided to the valley below sea level. Cone Peak at Big Sur was another conquest. Rick Sylvester scaled El Capitan in Yosemite and stepped into space beneath his Rogallo. He repeated the feat later but was detained by park rangers, who warned him not to try for three. Stopping high flights is like holding back the waves, however, and before long not one but six pilots evaded park officials early one morning and flew from El Capitan. One of these was Carol Boenish, a feminine leader in the movement and editor of USHGA's *Ground Skimmer* (she has since married Chris Price, another noted hang pilot).

Somewhere along the way, these safaris came to be known as Smokey-the-Bear trips, since they involved outwitting park rangers. The stance of officials is confused, since there seems to be no actual law against hang flying. "Violators" are sometimes charged with commercialism (taking photos to be sold), which *is* against the rules. Another charge is that hang flying is dangerous to practitioners and spectators alike, and thus cannot be tolerated in public areas.

Despite all odds, the glorious jaunts continue. Rich Matros and Zeke Finnery of San Diego, California, claimed, in 1973, to be the first to make international flights with their Rogallos. Launching from Tecate Peak near the Mexican border, they flew about a quarter of a mile into that country and then flew back to California. They apparently did not trigger any radar alarms, as no jet interceptors appeared to challenge them.

Elsewhere around the world hang pilots fly from volcanic craters in Hawaii and over Europe's rugged Alps. In the latter setting, American hang pilot Rudy Kishazy leaped from Mont Blanc in October of 1973, claiming an altitude-of-launch record of 13,152 feet. This seems to have established a world mark, but

Skier Rudy Kishazy made a spectacular glider-assisted leap on the way down Mont Blanc in France, setting a record of almost 16,000 feet. *Courtesy Delta Wing Kites*

there is always Mount Everest, the ultimate Smokey-the-Bear venture!

Stunting and outwitting Smokey are only two aspects of hang gliding and many former acrobats are turning to other endeavors. Among them is pioneer stunter Bob Wills, who went to Hawaii and set an endurance record of 8 hours 24 minutes on the steady winds along the *palis*. The mark was soon exceeded by John Hughes of Kauai, however. Flying at the Waimanalo site, he remained aloft with his Rogallo for 10 hours 5 minutes, lasting out some torrential rains and two hours of dark before the moon came up. Easing the jolt to Bob Wills was the fact that the new record was made with one of his Wills wing gliders.

The Great Hang Gliding Championships

As soon as there was more than one hang glider, it was inevitable that "fly-ins" be held. These early affairs were informal get-togethers for the benefit of pilots and spectators (photographers in particular). But soon they became formalized shows and many have become annual meets. The pioneering "Turkey Fly" and "Photo Fly" have been replaced by Kitty Hawk Hang Glider Day (at one of these in North Carolina, contestants tried to break the ancient Orville Wright endurance record of over ten minutes but nobody could stay up even a minute), the Octave Chanute Hang Gliding Meet, the Annual National Soaring and Hang Gliding Festival, World Professional Hang Gliding Championships, the Annual United States Hang Gliding Championships, the Annual Otto Lilienthal Memorial Hang Gliding Championships, and the Annual Francis M. Rogallo Hang Glider Meet.

Most contests feature such competition as spot landing or endurance flights, and the only prizes involved are gliders and other items raffled off to raise money. But some meets are professionally competitive, with cash awards for winners. A number of Americans journeyed to the Big White Mountain Hang Glider Meet sponsored by Labatts Brewery in Canada. Some of them won cash awards (a total of $5,000 was offered) and some saw their plastic Rogallo sails disintegrate in below freezing weather!

Big soaring has its Smirnoff Sailplane Derby, and hang gliding has been treated to the smaller scale Annie Green Springs Hang Glider Championships. Such commercialism is opposed by some purists in the sport, both from the standpoint of the money offered and the tie with alcoholic beverages.

A more traditional affair is the Annual Montgomery Glider Flight Competition. Entries must be built from the plans of the original craft that John J. Montgomery claimed to have flown for 600 feet in 1883. A prize of $1500 has been offered for the first hang glider to duplicate that flight on a slope of not more than 11 degrees. Wind speed must be between five and thirteen miles an hour. The glider must weigh at least 40 pounds and can

Mike Larson, who placed third in the First National Hang Gliding Championships, flies his Rogallo high above the scenic Colorado landscape. *Courtesy
Peter Menzel, Chandelle Corp.*

be towed by an assistant with a tow line no more than 10 feet long. No one had won this award by 1974, but attempts continue.

Competition is a big part of soaring—too big a part, according to some hang pilots. They argue forcefully that competition kills the joy of soaring, detracts from the beauty of free flight, and turns the pilot into a tense and anxious machine, who wins by being a computer with money enough to buy the latest fiberglass machine and the most sophisticated electronic equipment. Competition is thriving, nevertheless. While contests often seem but an excuse to get a lot of gliders together for a day or weekend of soaring, competition is undeniably part of the appeal. And the urge to win is clearly strong in many pilots. Even the Wright brothers felt the desire to establish records.

Pilot and crew carry a replica of Montgomery's first glider up the same hill from which the pioneering craft is said to have flown. *Photo by George Uveges*

Hanging Five

As hang gliding grew rapidly as a sport, it was obvious to those seriously concerned about it that there was a need for rules and regulations, much as such regimentation went against the grain of those who had turned to hang flying for its simplicity and freedom. Taras Kiceniuk, Sr., suggested several classes of hang gliding flight ranging from minimum free flight within a few feet of the ground through controlled soaring flight at altitudes less than 200 feet, to unlimited soaring flight in places and at times conventional sailplanes usually fly.

Following the lead of other organized sports, notably that of conventional soaring, USHGA has developed its Hang Badge Program, offering awards for completion of landmarks along the way toward hang gliding proficiency. These awards serve a double purpose. First, they reward, but they also insure that recipients acquire a knowledge of flight and safety. A brief description of the Hang Badge requirements is given here. Full official USHGA rules will be found on pages 141–144.

HANG ONE

Unassisted takeoff, safe straight flight, good landings, beginner hills in gentle conditions. Ground clearance up to 20 feet. Know material in *Guide to Rogallo Flight—Basic,* excluding turns. Must be signed by a USHGA-recognized instructor.

HANG TWO

Planned flight paths with "S" turns at least 90 degrees azimuth for approach control, landing within 50 feet of spot, ground clearance of at least 50 feet, smooth winds to 18 mph, gusty to 11 mph. Know all material in *Guide to Rogallo Flight—Basic.* Must be signed by a USHGA-recognized instructor.

HANG THREE

Sets of linked "S" turns, both steep and gentle, figure eights around pylons, spot landings within 30 feet, repeated ground clearance of 200 feet. Must be competent in winds up to 15 mph with gusts. Able to discuss turns, stalls, approach control, rights of way, reflex and stability, rotors and diurnal winds, FAA definition of control zones and airways. Must be signed by a USHGA observer. If no previous Hang Two Rating, must be signed by USHGA-recognized instructor.

HANG FOUR

Repeated flights over five minutes' duration. Repeated flights with over 300-feet terrain clearance in conditions requiring aggressive control application with confidence. Soaring flight above low point for at least one minute. 180-degree entry turns in both directions, gentle to steep 180-degree linked "S" turns in both directions. Landings within 20 feet of spot. Must possess or demonstrate Hang Three Rating, including instructor requirement. Must be signed by USHGA observer. Additional Hang Four special skills: 360's, turbulence, high altitude, cliff launch (calm and windy), and cross-country. Must be signed by USHGA observer.

HANG FIVE

Hang Four with no limitations. Earned reputation for good judgment. Must be signed by three USHGA observers.

Winning Silver Badges

In conventional soaring, a series of badges awarded for increasingly difficult flights add interest to the sport. A, B, and C badges are not too difficult and come almost as a matter of course after a fair number of flights. The C Badge calls for an hour's flight above release point, and many hang glider pilots have unofficially qualified for this one. The next step is the Silver C Badge. To earn this, a pilot must make a flight of five hours or more duration, climb 1,000 meters (3,281 feet) above his release point and fly a distance of 50 kilometers (31.1 miles) in a straight line.

These are no small feats, even in a sailplane costing thousands of dollars and equipped with rather sophisticated instruments. Perhaps 30,000 Americans have soared but less than 2600 had won the Silver C by mid-1974. For hang pilots, in craft costing a few hundred dollars, to achieve the Silver Badge sounds as remote as going to the moon did prior to the 1960s. But men did reach the moon—and very likely hang pilots will be garnering Silver Badges shortly. As a matter of fact, in May of 1974 officials of The Soaring Society of America announced that two hang glider applications for Silver Badge endurance legs were being processed and that both flights "easily exceeded the required five hours as substantiated by barograms and the certification of an official SSA observer." For comparison, Otto Lilienthal amassed a *total* flying time of about five hours in five years of flying!

A hang glider can probably stay aloft as long as any conventional sailplane, if such endurance is important enough to its pilot. Hang gliders have flown above 10,000 feet. This suggests that hang pilots may gain 3,000 meters of altitude and earn Gold Badge altitude legs, and maybe 5,000 meters for Diamond altitude. This would require the additon of an oxygen tank to the hang glider, of course.

Rigid-wing hang gliders cruise at 20 to 25 miles an hour, and at that speed a flight of even 187 miles (Gold distance) is a possibility on a very good soaring day. Where is the hang pilot who doesn't thrill at the prospect of flying such a distance? More modest cross-country flights have already been made.

With his short flights to Turf Sailport behind him, Mark Clarkson improved his thermaling technique and flew from Shaw Butte to Pinnacle Peak one afternoon. This was more than 15 miles and about half the distance required for the Silver distance leg. Within a few months an American hang pilot had exceeded Clarkson's unofficial record by flying his Rogallo a distance of 11¼ miles along a ridge in New Zealand and the same distance back for a total of 22½ miles.

For cross-country flying, an altimeter is a must to judge how far one can go after climbing in a thermal. The variometer makes it easier to climb in thermals, since the instrument tells instantly whether the glider is going up or down. Designed for conventional cockpits, such instruments tend to be bulky by hang glider standards, but demand has produced miniature models that take only a little space. In fact, there is talk of using

Mark Clarkson flies the *Quicksilver*, in which he has climbed more than a mile high, flown for longer than five hours and for a distance of fifteen miles. *Courtesy Mark Clarkson*

only the audio unit, a sound signal that increases in frequency with increasing lift. Thus an earplug would give the pilot the information he needs, eliminating the need to look at the instrument.

Instruments represent a crossroads of vital significance in the sport of hang gliding, for its great initial appeal was in being simple and uncluttered by equipment and instruments. In fact, some hang pilots flatly refuse to consider such things as airspeed indicators, altimeters, compasses, or variometers. If they wanted to be instrument readers they would fly sailplanes, they protest.

It will be interesting to see what happens in this confrontation between eco-flight purist and instrument technologist. Surely a bare minimum of equipment makes hang gliding more fun. But where will it stop? If a little is good, wouldn't a lot be better? Already there is a division between those who favor body shifting and those who prefer movable controls. The latter group is more likely to adopt such additional complexities and evolve toward what is already referred to as the ultralight sailplane. This craft is much like conventional sailplanes except for its very low weight and slow speed.

9

Toward the Human-powered Airplane!

Obviously, hang gliding is only scratching the surface of a whole new era of flight—something described as "supersoarability," using ultralight sailplanes. Conventional soaring craft fly at speeds from 50 to more than 100 miles an hour and still achieve flat glides. Suppose one could achieve a 20- or even a 30-1 glide in a refinement of the hang glider, at speeds of about 30 miles an hour? And a sink rate only about one-fourth that of the conventional fiberglass bird? Such floating flight might be the ultimate joy of soaring.

For many Rogallo purists such talk is treason—the proposed craft would only be a very light sailplane! Instead of four or more pounds per square foot of wing area, the ultralight would weigh about two pounds per square foot. It would float like a zephyr on the faintest upcurrents, instead of requiring strong lift as do most hang gliders.

From Bamboo Butterfly to Thistledown

Richard Miller, who pioneered the whole business of hang gliding with his floppy *Bamboo Butterfly* in 1965, has proposed an ultralight design called *Thistledown*, a tailless flying wing, maneuvered by body English on the part of its pilot, plus minimum control surfaces. Although *Thistledown* would have an enclosed fuselage and a landing wheel, it would take off without benefit of air tow, winch, or auto launch, simply by having wing runners push it from a windswept hill.

Miller's dream craft would use a long narrow wing, with an area of only 104 square feet. With a fifty-foot span it would be almost exactly the size of the Standard *Libelle*, a competition-type German sailplane popular around the world. But there would be a world of performance difference between *Thistledown* and its heavier cousin. The *Libelle* has a sink rate of 120 feet a minute at a speed of about 60 miles an hour. This works out to a remarkable 38-1 glide. *Thistledown* would also have a glide of 38-1—but at 30 miles an hour, and with a sink rate of only 60 feet per minute! Obviously it could climb in lift too weak to keep the much heavier *Libelle* airborne.

The design philosophy for modern sailplanes has been to make them heavy and fast for high cross-country speed. So the idea of an ultralight flying machine floating along at half the speed of a competition sailplane suggests pathetic speeds between point A and point B. However, Miller has carefully worked out the comparative performances of the *Libelle* and his dream *Thistledown* and the results are surprising. On an eight-hour cross-country flight in very weak conditions, *Thistledown* could actually beat the *Libelle*, averaging 36 miles an hour to the heavier craft's 30 miles an hour. This because *Thistledown* would spend only an hour in climbing (because of its much faster climb and much flatter glide). On a stronger day the *Libelle* would fly faster than *Thistledown*, but the ultralight's performance would improve, too. Flown with a moderate tailwind, it might achieve sufficient speed for flights of Diamond distance: 500 kilometers or 311 miles.

Should it prove possible to decrease the sink rate by half again, to a barely perceptible 30 feet per minute, Miller calculates that such a craft could fly cross-country without ever stopping to climb in updrafts! It would encounter lift often enough and gain enough altitude without turning to offset its descent between areas of lift.

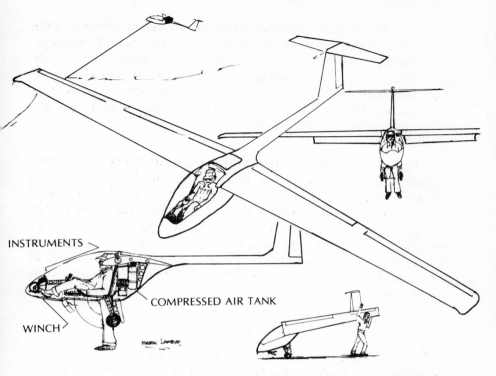

INSTRUMENTS

COMPRESSED AIR TANK

WINCH

MARK LAMBIE

Jack Lambie, designer-builder of the pioneering *Hang Loose*, foresees sleek, self-launched hang gliders that will fly for hundreds of miles. *Courtesy Mark Lambie*, Ground Skimmer

Craft like *Thistledown* have flown only in fancy, but the evolution of Taras Kiceniuk's tailless *Icarus* hang gliders is taking them toward just such a supersoarer. With its swept monoplane wing and underslung pilot, *Icarus V* differs from *Thistledown* mainly in that it has no enclosed pod for the pilot. It also differs, of course, in the fact that its glide is a modest 10-1, rather than the theoretical 38-1 of *Thistledown*. And *Icarus* sinks at 3.5 feet per second instead of only 1 foot per second. But the promise is there for those who seek supersoarability.

Jack Lambie, who designed *Hang Loose*, also has suggested a new dimension for hang gliding. As a symposium speaker at Northrop Institute of Technology, he proposed stronger, slightly faster gliders built of exotic material (he jokingly called it "unattainium"). And in the June 1974 *Soaring* magazine he described a flight of the future in one of these supersoarers:

. . . In the early morning darkness we pull our folded-wing craft to the top of a 6000-foot mountain near Tehachapi, California. We have a brief, busy time while we attach the long, slim boron fiberglass matrix shell to the foam-and-boron fiberglass fuselages. We don our battery packs (for heated flying suits) and tiny radios, then stretch out the 50-foot-long shock cords. . . .

These shock cords, resembling the old-time bungee launchers common in the early days of gliding, get Lambie's heavier and sleeker ultralight into the air. Once airborne, the pilot swings up inside the fuselage, reels in the shock cord, and retracts the landing gear to make the craft as streamlined as today's sailplanes. With its high performance it would be capable of traversing the continent in comfortable hops of several hundred miles a day, stopping at airports, ski resorts, or just about anywhere.

Pedal Power!

One obvious problem of the ultralight machine is that it has a much higher weight than a Rogallo. It is one thing to put on a set of wings weighing 40 to 50 pounds and leap from a cliff for take-off. Doing the same thing with a machine weighing 200 pounds is far beyond human ability. Since self-launching seems a must for hang gliding, the big machine is doomed unless a satisfactory substitute for running can be worked out. Boeing engineer Jack Olson has suggested a possible alternative. There are many places where smooth, rolling hills abound, and where a wheeled glider could coast downward until it reached flying speed. Then it could leave the hillside, gain altitude, and fly about, perhaps at last coming in for a landing back on top of the hill. Olson's idea also includes the production of standard wing and tail assemblies and basic frame fuselages, letting builders dress up the front end with accessories to suit their fancy. This sort of customizing appeals to dune-buggy builders, and he reasons that it might also interest hang pilots.

Foot launching is a generally accepted requirement of hang gliding, however, and purists fight the idea of wheeled landing

This pusher-type kite was built under government contract. *Courtesy Ryan Aeronautical Company*

gear and react in horror to suggestions for adding pedal drive to the landing wheel. However, riding a bike is done with the legs and feet, and no one objects to cycling as an ecosport. What matter if the hang pilot runs on his legs or pedals with them to get up speed for a rolling launch from the top of a hill? Which leads to the idea of designing the ultralight so that its wings can be folded and the whole thing pedaled to and from soaring sites.

Richard Miller goes further and suggests ways of reducing the ultralight's sink rate to zero feet per minute; sustained flight with no lift! He would do this by adding bicycle pedals attached to a pusher propeller installed on *Thistledown's* streamlined pod fuselage. Pedaling at maximum power, the pilot could achieve level flight for short periods. But much less effort, easily managed for long periods of time, could reduce sink rate to only about 60 feet a minute. Flying this "hang cycle" would be something like riding a bicycle on hilly country. Except that in the aerial case you pedal going downhill, and coast going uphill on rising air.

Self-Powered Flight at Last!

Some dedicated idealists fault the Wright brothers for spoiling the beautiful concept of bird flight by adding an engine. And much of the appeal of hang gliding is indeed on the ecological and aesthetic level: A self-launched machine, producing no pollutants of any kind—noise, smoke, or noxious gases. Yet early in the renaissance of self-flight there came those dabblers who insisted on adding power.

The thought of mechanical power added to a beautiful self-soaring machine turns off most hang pilots, however. Which leaves one last hope: the self-launched, *self-powered* craft. This of course is the oldest idea of all, for Daedalus and Icarus flapped their wings to *climb* through Aegean skies, and Leonardo da Vinci devoted his genius to trying to make a muscle-powered ornithopter carry a human through the air. All through aviation history a long succession of would-be birdmen, ranging from serious scientists to kooks, have flapped and cranked and fluttered in glides of varying steepness. But in recent decades some have actually succeeded in taking off from level ground and staying aloft for appreciable distances!

Pedaling into the Blue

Even though the Wrights had shown convincingly that the propeller was the better way for aircraft, the flapping-wing idea died hard. In 1929 gliding was very popular in Germany because of the tight restrictions imposed on that country against building engine-powered craft following World War I. Nobody had restricted *human* power, however, so Alexander Lippish got busy and produced a clean-looking monoplane with flexible wing panels that could be flapped up and down by a pilot pedaling energetically. Launched with rubber shock cord (the standard method for gliders in those days) the wing flapper reportedly made flights as long as 300 yards, and at least some of this distance must have come from muscle power. This was a human-*assisted* glide at best, and not truly powered flight.

The seeds were sown, however, and in 1933 German publisher

Oskar Ursinus offered a cash prize of 500 marks for the first human-powered flight of one kilometer around two pylons placed 400 meters apart. By 1935 Helmut Haessler and Franz Villinger, engineers for the German Junkers firm, built and flew such a craft, called the *Mufli*, using a propeller turned by pedals. Although it did not achieve the 1,000-meter distance specified, the clever design flew 790 yards after an assisted takeoff and was awarded a consolation prize as the best effort at the trials.

Interest spread to Italy, and when a prize was offered there, Enea Bossi and Vittorio Bonomi designed and built a pedal-powered airplane. Appropriately named the *Pedaliante*, this twin-propeller craft was launched with shock cord and flew about 980 yards. This flight included two 90° turns, mostly at a sustained altitude of about 10 feet. An innovation was the inclusion of landing wheels, also driven by the pedals that turned the propellers. Claims were made that the *Pedaliante* actually took off on pedal-power but this has been disputed. Built far stronger than necessary, the craft weighed more than two pounds to the square foot and it was a tribute to its designers' skill that it flew at all. Unfortunately both the *Mufli* and *Pedaliante* were destroyed in World War II, and that was the end of human-powered flight for almost twenty years.

Henry Kremer and His Prize

It is interesting to note that most progress with human-powered craft has come with the promise of cash awards. This had happened in Germany and Italy. It happened again in England. In 1957 a Man-Powered Aircraft Group of the Royal Aeronautical Society of England was formed, and at the same time industrialist Henry Kremer offered the sizeable prize of £5000 for the first aircraft to make a human-powered flight in a figure eight around two pylons placed a half mile apart.

Understandably the Kremer Prize created a furor, and financial assistance was given to several interested design teams. These included groups at Southampton University and the Hatfield Club. At Southampton design work began in July of 1960 and the SUMPAC (Southampton University Man-Powered Air Craft) was actually begun in January of 1961. The large frail craft was completed in the late fall of 1961 and readied for flight.

SUMPAC's builder waited impatiently for a day of absolutely still air. Then, as the first trials began, a series of minor mishaps frayed tense nerves. The bicycle drive chain came off its gears. The wheel went flat, and the frame bent when the pilot put pressure on the pedals! After all these flaws had been fixed, another attempt was made. This time, in a high-speed taxi test, SUMPAC ground-looped off the runway and damaged the nose-wheel and the front-end structure.

Finally, on November 9 at 4:30 in the afternoon, with calm conditions, Derek Piggott, a noted sailplane pilot, climbed into the cockpit and pedaled hopefully down the runway at Lasham Gliding Centre. SUMPAC lifted easily, climbed about 6 feet high, and flew for 50 yards before touching down again. For the first time in history a man had definitely taken off and flown under his own power. Success in winning the Kremer Prize seemed assured at this point, and this feeling was strengthened when SUMPAC quickly followed up with much better flights. On November 24 and 25, further flights pushed the mark up to a remarkable 350-yard flight lasting 30 seconds. In 1962 this distance was nearly doubled with a flight of 650 yards. However, the competition had meanwhile caught up and passed SUMPAC.

The Hatfield Club entry did not get airborne until after SUMPAC, flying first on November 16, 1961. But it came on much faster than its competitor. Before 1961 ended, the *Puffin* had flown 700 yards in straight flight. Early flights were made by test pilots from the De Havilland Aircraft Company, but in May of 1962 nonpilot John Wimpenny, leader of the design and construction group, climbed in and flew *Puffin* the remarkable distance of 993 yards. Since the much heavier Italian craft had flown almost this far in 1936, it might seem that a quarter of a century had brought little progress. The important difference, of course, was that *Puffin* had taken off with *human* power, and was not catapulted aloft to make a slow glide back to earth.

To win the Kremer Prize required flying only about twice as far as had already been flown, and 90° turns had been demonstrated. Predictions were confidently made that the prize

England's *Puffin II* passes a marker pole under its own power at an altitude of 17 feet. *Courtesy Keith Sherwin*

was in the bag, the only question being which contender would do it first. It proved to be a far more difficult feat, and both SUMPAC and *Puffin* crashed in later flights without having come close to achieving figure eight flights. SUMPAC ended its distinguished career when a professional cyclist, attempting a record flight, stalled in a wind gust and crashed from 30 feet. *Puffin* was tossed about by turbulence at a lower altitude and collided with a runway light. Lightly built as it was, the frail craft crumpled like tissue-paper kites.

There were other disappointments. *Mayfly*, the hope of the Southend group funded by the Royal Aeronautical Society, *didn't* fly. Neither did the Woodford machine, which burned when its hangar caught fire. The *Weybridge* MPA, and the mighty *Toucan*, with two pilots and a wingspan of 123 feet, fell farther and farther behind schedule. Wimpenny's flight had been just a few yards short of the magic distance of 1000 yards, and it seemed that someone would soon exceed this mark, since it was so quickly achieved in the first modern attempt at human-powered flight. But it was a decade before Wimpenny's mark was topped.

On June 29, 1972, the British *Jupiter* (rebuilt from the fire-damaged Woodford machine) was wheeled onto the runway of Benson Airfield at Oxfordshire, England. The pilot, RAF flight lieutenant John Potter, weighed more than *Jupiter*, which tipped the scales at only 140 pounds. Lieutenant Potter got airborne at 1:47 in the afternoon and stayed aloft for the record distance of 1,171 yards, 2 feet, and 10 inches. The craft made a total of some 100 flights in a few months, boosting the record to 1,355 yards, but could not negotiate the tough and tricky Kremer course. Even the simpler task of flying a series of gentle turns about three pylons placed one quarter of a mile apart, landing, turning around, and flying back, has not been achieved.

Since the original offer of £5,000 made by Henry Kremer, the amount has been boosted several times, until at this writing it is equivalent to $129,000! Should this fail to produce a flight around the required course, it would seem that the feat may not be possible using present technologies, materials, and approach.

Most of the human-powered experiments have taken place in England, and one commentator thinks he knows why, "It would be difficult to imagine a more typically British venture: It is dangerous, curious, impractical and probably impossible—and of course, taken terribly seriously." However, MPAs have been built and are being built in a number of other countries. Japanese enthusiasts built a series of four craft called *Linnets*, which flew, and the Sato-Maeda design also got off the ground under its own power. Austria's *Malliga* flew about 150 yards in 1967. Canada has built a two-man craft but no flight results have been reported.

United States efforts include the McAvoy *MPA-1*, built at Georgia Tech in 1963 but damaged in a ground accident before

Flight Lt. John Potter flew *Jupiter* a distance of 1,355 yards. (The nose canopy is removed in this picture to show the bicycle mechanism.) *Courtesy Scientific American*

being flown. More recently, both Massachusetts Institute of Technology and Northrop Institute of Technology have been working on human-powered airplanes. Both of these are two-person configurations.

Keith Sherwin, an Englishman who wrote the book *Man-Powered Flight,* heads a group approaching the task in a simpler way. Using the remains of the ill-fated *Puffin,* these experimenters have produced a craft with a span of only 50 feet, capable of short training flights of 100 yards or more. Dr. Lippisch, who designed the German wing-flapper in 1929, points out that "it is better to be content with the low-hanging grapes first, and then to try to climb higher for the larger

MIT's human-powered aircraft is designed for a two-person team. *Courtesy Massachusetts Institute of Technology*

bunches." Such research might achieve two ends. First would be the accomplishment of sport human-powered aircraft. It might also eventually produce smaller, more maneuverable craft to belatedly win the Kremer Award.

Giant, superlight, supersophisticated craft are far too costly and too hard to handle to be considered sport flying machines. However, we now have very lightweight craft flying in slope winds and thermals. Converting the best of these to a human-powered craft able in a brief spurt to climb into rising air seems a probable achievement.

John McMasters, an ultralight enthusiast who has followed human-powered flight closely for years, wrote the following fanciful prediction in *Soaring* magazine in February, 1972:

Pedaling gently at first, you increase effort until you hit your pace. The craft accelerates slowly but finally the light skipping of its wheels tells you it's airborne in the ground effect. You continue pedaling strongly until the "runway thermal" takes effect, permitting you to taper off your exertion and concentrate on flying. As you near the end of the runway it is necessary to pedal harder again while you bank gently around for another pass over the runway's long narrow thermal. Careful now—not too much bank until you're higher! Even at a ground speed of less than 15 mph a groundloop is costly. After several passes you have gained enough altitude to quit pedaling altogether and concentrate on thermaling, moving about the area with as much freedom as a large bird, leaving the earth's labyrinth far below.

A flight of fancy today? Sure. But tomorrow the man-powered self-launching sailplane could become as familiar as the 1-26.

Even this happy state of affairs may not be the ultimate. Mc-Masters, and others, have talked for some years of the solar-powered sailplane—a lightweight craft whose wings are covered with solar cells to drive a small electric motor and large-diameter

This homebuilt craft, with Ken Privett at the controls, is an experimental model that didn't quite get off the ground. *Courtesy* Low and Slow

propeller! While such a bank of solar cells at today's prices would cost more than the Kremer Award, with all the emphasis on solar energy development that is going on, prices may come down to a reasonable figure. Then you can wheel out your solar soarer, pedal down the runway to assist the propeller, climb on sun power, shut down the motor, and soar away on a thermal! And the *Bamboo Butterfly* will have evolved into a solar soarer, harnessing the sun that toppled Icarus from the sky so long ago.

10
Hang Gliding Comes of Age

THOSE INVOLVED IN any sport tend to congregate, but hang gliding enthusiasts in particular seem to need to get together. The movement began in Southern California. This was logical, since Richard Miller and other pioneers did their test flying there, but Francis Rogallo has commented jokingly that there must be something in the air around Los Angeles conducive to hang gliding. Rogallo lives near Kitty Hawk, North Carolina, and has seen the activity grow there, too. But the great push did begin in California and spread quickly to the rest of the country by newsletter and word-of-mouth descriptions of the ultimate in sports.

The Self-Soar Association

The Self-Soar Association was started by Joe Faust, a former Olympic high jumper who saw big things in hang gliding. Richard Miller had originated an underground newsletter called *Low, Slow and Out of Control*, and at Miller's urging, Faust took it over and has published it for several years as a labor of love, with the help of his wife Joanne and their children. It documents the hang gliding movement, and poetically explains the philosophy and goals of the sport.

An engineer who studied at UCLA, Faust found work in the aircraft industry unrewarding and gave it up after three years to devote himself to promoting hang gliding. This he has done with missionary zeal, in the air and at his typewriter. In the first issue of this newsletter he commented:

> Levitation is one of the many transcendental *L&S* topics. The flight of vision, image, thought, love, and creativity are others. These motorless flights are quiet, non-fueled, winged, and expansive. Poets, mystics, lovers, and soaring and gliding people have much in common. We hope to investigate the descriptions of how man will fly in heaven, how angels fly, how the winged-footed Mercury flew. Transcendental flight considerations will certainly not keep us away from returning to mechanical flight. Each area can induce progress in the other.

The Self-Soar Association remains an informal group of enthusiasts who pay a token entry fee and dues, and receive "Otto" numbers (honoring Otto Lilienthal, who himself was assigned Otto #1). Self-Soar has no officers other than president Joe Faust, holds no meetings, and serves primarily to keep up interest and to spread information through *Low and Slow* and its companion *Hang Glider Weekly*. With membership comes a "Welcome to self-soaring, that very special art, science, and sport of flying yourself fuel-lessly." The author's card, issued in May of 1974, is Otto #12,236.

The United States Hang Gliding Association

In December 1971 the Peninsula Hang Glider Club was formed with about 25 members. Membership grew so fast that it soon became the Southern California Hang Gliding Association, or SCHGA. Within two years membership was close to 5000 with representation all over the United States. In fact, nearly three-fourths of the members were in other states, and 5 percent were Canadians and other foreign nationals. As a result,

Hang glider contests have gained popularity rapidly. Here a contestant in the 1974 Otto Lilienthal Meet comes in for a landing after a long flight from the hills above Sylmar. This site has since been closed. *Photo by Dan Halacy*

SCHGA directors voted in December of 1973 to change the name to the United States Hang Gliding Association. Membership topped 10,000 by October 1974. In contrast, the Soaring Society of America, in 40 years, built a total membership of only about 12,500.

USHGA publishes *Ground Skimmer*, which features editorials, articles, and photos, plus advertising. A number of other publications also report on the hang gliding scene. There are dozens of regional hang gliding clubs in the United States and abroad, and many of them publish newsletters or magazines. Some hang glider manufacturers also have publications, and a wealth of material has been printed on the sport. Clubs and publications are listed on pages 145–149.

Trouble in Paradise

The Soaring Society of America, formed in the 1930s, viewed hang gliders with raised eyebrows when such craft first began invading air space. Strong disagreement soon developed between those who favored hang gliders and those who thought them a menace to soaring. Some critics recalled that SSA was formed in the first place to offset the bad effects of scatter-brained glider fliers (including some hang gliding types). Who needed an avalanche of wild-eyed and irresponsible hang pilots who would give *all* soaring a bad image and kill themselves in the process?

Many soaring people, however, were enthusiastic about the new sport. Richard Miller, a leading exponent of hang gliding, was at one time the editor of *Soaring* magazine, official journal of sailplane flying. Lloyd Licher, executive director of the Soaring Society of America, also proclaimed his interest in hang gliding as a responsible sport. When he was elected president of SCHGA, some SSA members demanded that he be chastised, or even relieved of his job. Cooler heads prevailed and Licher continued to wear two hats, judiciously changing to his hang gliding helmet after hours.

The Executive Board of SSA pondered the problem and the result was a position paper taking up the question of "whether or not SSA should go hang." The most nagging concern was the fact that within a short time far more sets of plans for hang gliders had been sold than there were sailplanes in the United States! Obviously, many of the would-be builders had no intention of submitting their homemade craft for FAA inspection and licensing, or of obtaining an FAA student pilot certificate before teaching themselves to fly in aircraft costing less than $100 to build.

The position paper also criticized designs that depended on an "extremely agile pilot for what little stability they could claim," and further argued that some "lacked the elementary structural requirements of a breezeworthy umbrella, much less those of a man-carrying aircraft." Such designers, SSA claimed, were motivated more by synthetic nostalgia for an aeronautical past than by seventy years of technical progress in flight. This disregard for safety might result in an epidemic of accidents and the FAA would then ask SSA how a responsible aviation organization could let such a thing happen.

At the same time, the SSA recognized a dilemma. Many of its graybeard members themselves bragged of having jumped off chicken houses in homemade flying machines and launched from cliffs in none-too-airworthy craft. Now this same natural exuberance was being challenged by a new generation, which could draw on a wealth of new materials, techniques, and designs. Properly handled, the wave of experimentation could lead to improvements in both categories of soaring.

Nevertheless, on grounds of safety, SSA had to deplore the inherent dangers in hang gliding. Because of the great interest in the sport, and thus the great potential danger to many participants, SSA felt a duty to attempt to regulate in the interests of safety. To implement this, SSA's responsibility was suggested as one of "welcoming hang gliding into the 1970s."

Specifically the SSA recommended encouragement of the development of ultralight gliders (as they preferred to call the new craft) in legal channels as provided by FAA. SSA members, chapters, and SSA affiliated commercial operators were asked to assist hang glider beginners, since they would be obvious candidates for conventional soaring because of the "relatively low payoff in the flight of low and slow gliders." Advertising of hang gliders would be accepted in *Soaring* magazine only if it included instructions for licensing through the FAA and specified that pilots hold appropriate FAA pilot certificates before making solo flights. In addition, SSA's Technical Board would be bolstered by an Ultralight Committee, and SSA would seriously consider adding a chapter on hang gliding to its *Soaring Handbook*.

Joe Faust responded quickly and forthrightly in *Low and Slow*, asking why there was ever any doubt about SSA's "going hang," since it was originally chartered to promote *all* forms of gliding safely. As to the business of following FAA procedures,

Faust stated, "When we intend to hang our toes over cities and in the airspace that would be shared by other aircraft, then let us tie in with the FAA closely, but not before."

Responding to the report that more hang glider plans had been sold than there were sailplanes, *Low and Slow* pointed out that actually there were more *completed* hang gliders than sailplanes—by a factor of five!

"It is amazing," noted Faust, "that only two to three thousand sailplanes make up the gliding movement that is called the SSA—for 220 million people! That comes to one sailplane for each 110,000 people. I wonder how many people out of a random selection have desired deeply to be able to share the Earth with the birds in a simple mode of being in flight."

As to the dangers of learning to fly hang gliders, *Low and Slow* commented, "Learning to land is fun and is something that often provides some bruises for the beginner; but the experience is not as treacherous as a youngster learning to land his first two-wheeled bike."

In its position paper, *Low and Slow* cited a comment from FAA officials to the effect that "We have more important things to do than watch you guys meander around the hillsides." Why should federal money be spent to investigate and license the millions of "non-bothering craft" that people will use for picnic-type flying? While FAA seemed to share the feelings of most self-soarers that hang gliders need not be regulated like other aircraft, hang gliding people had moved on their own toward far stronger craft than the first floppy Rogallos that had horrified some SSA leaders. In fact, most commercial hang gliders are designed and built with a safety factor comparable to conventional sailplanes. Arguments against inspections and other regulations referred to what hang glider people call Class 1 and Class 2 flight. Class 3 is another matter, because it does share the same airspace and fly over the same terrain as other, licensed aircraft. Such flight should be regulated, *Low and Slow* agreed.

The position assumed by SSA as of early 1974 was that it would not actively foster hang gliding but encourage it to proceed on its own as a separate sport. However, the society stood ready to advise when requested, and *Soaring's* pages began to

Mark Clarkson, Arizona's leading hang glider pilot, rests with friends in the shade of a Rogallo kite after a day of flying near Prescott. *Photo by Dan Halacy*

describe hang glider activities, ultralight seminars, and other items still considered questionable by some SSA members.

How Safe?

In spite of SSA's concern about how safe hang gliding is, the new sport was relatively safe through its first few years. Discounting fatalities caused by towing behind cars or boats, there was not a death attributable to hang gliding until 1972, when Ed Gardia died in a crash. (A memorial award was created in his name, honoring the person who has done most for the sport each year. Volmer Jensen received it in 1972 and Francis Rogallo in 1973.)

With the rapid growth of hang gliding, however, six pilots were killed in 1973, and 1974 seemed to be living up to the fears of critics with a dozen deaths by midyear. Ignorance, carelessness, and recklessness seemed to be involved, particularly the latter. Such stunts as standing upright in the trapeze bar were cited as horrible examples of how to finish off the sport before it was ten years old. Yet recklessness was not the whole story. Eric Wills, whose brothers Bob and Chris had become legends, died attempting a 360° turn too close to a mountain. His parents wrote a plea in *Ground Skimmer* for more flight instruction and greater stress on safety. Ironically the increase in deaths came after initiation of strict safety rules and a self-regulation approach that all agreed was needed.

In May of 1974 the FAA announced tentative regulations for the sport, surely with an eye on the mounting fatalities. The voluntary safety standards suggested by FAA included an altitude limit of 500 feet above the ground, avoidance of airports without traffic controls, no cloud flying, respect for prohibited or restricted areas unless prior permission is granted, and observance of a 100-foot clearance from buildings, populated places, and groups of people. Furthermore, the FAA pointed out that hang gliders do *not* have right-of-way priority with regard to other aircraft. Conventional sailplanes do have the right-of-way over powered aircraft. Announcing that it hoped mandatory rules

·would not be needed, the FAA stated that it would continue to monitor the growth of hang gliding, and particularly its safety record, to determine further action.

Where to Fly?

A growing problem for hang pilots is where to fly. As the number of hang gliders increased and flights went higher and longer, many private and public sites were closed to the craft. Playa del Rey, site of Richard Miller's historic flights, was long ago put off limits for hang gliders. Then Torrance Beach was restricted, followed by dozens of other sites, including USHGA's own Hang Glider Park at Sylmar, California. Hang pilots using Warren Dunes State Park in Michigan were told by park rangers that the first injury to pilots or spectators would also be the last. With mock seriousness a club newsletter instructed injured pilots to crawl quickly into the brush! Another suggestion was the use of tie-dyed camouflage wing sails. Even where flying is still permitted, problems increase. A recent addition to hang glider woes was a sightseeing helicopter giving passengers a close view of Rogallos in flight.

In spite of their ability to land in small areas, it is inevitable that hang gliders gradually will be banned from populated areas and forced to travel farther to find available sites. Just as surely, certain areas will develop as strictly hang gliding turf. Escape Country, 50 miles southeast of Los Angeles, may be one such spot. Here hang gliders have been welcomed for some time by a sympathetic management.

USHGA's Chuck Kocsis Fund has been set up for the preservation of flying sites, a cause Kocsis was much interested in up to the time of his death in a hang glider accident. The money will be used to educate the public about hang gliding, to post insurance and bonds for flying sites and to fence and otherwise maintain such sites, and to conduct a national survey of available sites. The motto of the new movement is SOAR, Save Our Airspace Resources.

Onward and Upward

Hang gliding is coming of age, but its maturity is beset by many problems. Involving as it does some element of risk, responsibilities are serious and failure to meet them can slow the sport or even bring it to a halt. As in any sport, there is a small fringe of undesirables. All are permitted to fly hang gliders, but not all are qualified to do so, any more than all can safely ride surfboards or motorcycles. There are problems ahead for individuals and for hang gliding as an organized group. But it seems likely that the young men and women who have solved the centuries-old problem of human flight will likewise succeed in solving the lesser problems of regulation and public relations.

Hang gliding can be reasonably safe, just as any flying can be. At the Fourth Annual Otto Lilienthal Memorial Contest, more than 300 entrants made more than 1,200 flights without an injury. As pleased officials announced, the only accident victim was a small boy who fell off his bike. Either through self-regulation or governmental action, safety will be achieved, although there will always be the few who cannot be bound by such rules and will hurt themselves and sometimes others. Crowding is a symptom of the times, and the crowded sky is an old complaint. But neither the sky nor the landscape is so crowded that there is not room for self-soarers and their winged craft, for theirs is a beautiful sport.

Appendixes

U.S. Hang Gliding Association Hang Badge Program

HANG ONE

1. Unassisted takeoff: just that—no keel push.
   Shouldn't jump onto the glider.
2. Safe straight flight:
   a) Minor corrections in flight so that pilot lands into the wind on his feet.
   b) Should control the airspeed without undue overcontrol.
3. The material in the *Guide* should be discussed enough so that observer is convinced that the pilot understands it.
4. Should feel confident that he can fly another beginner hill without causing troubles for others.
5. Should be able to set up and check his own glider.

HANG TWO

1. "S" Turns: Alternating left and right turns with at least one of each. They should be smooth and without very much speed change. Pilot should never have to roll out of a turn because of either too much or too little airspeed.
2. It should be evident that flyer can use the turns to set up a spot landing.
3. When discussing the material in *Guide*, observer should be sure to see that flyer understands the proper use of pitch and roll in turns.

1. When a pilot receives a Hang Three Rating, he will then be going out to other sites.

2. Linked "S" Turns:

   a) These are "S" turns in which the pilot rolls right out of one turn into the next without hesitation at the level point. Both turns will have the same degree of bank and same airspeed. As the glider rolls from one to the other, there must be no apparent pitching up or down.

   b) A gentle turn is one in which very little positive pitch is necessary and roll control is required throughout. A steep turn is one in which little roll control is maintained, but definite and aggressive positive pitch is required.

   c) Note whether the steepness of the turn changes during the turn. The turn must be entered smoothly to a definite bank angle and turn rate, and these must be held until completion without appreciable speed gain or loss.

   d) No slipping or skidding.

   e) All "S" turns for Hang Three must be 180-degree azimuth, ± 10 degrees.

   f) "S" turns should be accomplished across the wind with all turns into the wind.

3. Figure Eights:

   a) The pilot will choose two points which are across the wind. The wind must be sufficient to cause definite ground drift. The pilot will fly toward the midpoint between the pylons; at the proper time he will turn across the wind to enter the figure eight with an upwind turn. The crosswind leg is used to help establish the ground drift information.

   b) The turns in the eight will be gentle to medium as required.

   c) Fly the turns so that they describe a constant radius ground track around the pylons.

   d) The turns must be altered smoothly as they are flown around the pylons.

   e) The cross in the eight should consist of straight line segments, which should be entered confidently and require only very minor corrections for drift changes so that the entry to the second turn of the eight is at the same radius as the other turn.

   f) The important points to consider are precision of correction for wind drift and the smoothness shown while turning.

   g) Height will reduce the accuracy possible in judging distance around the turn and should be allowed for both from the point of view of the pilot and observer.

4. The observer must make sure that the pilot really understands the oral questions. You are not grading him; he either knows or not. None of the subjects are unimportant.

HANG FOUR

1. Here is where the pressures will really be brought to bear on the observer. There are pilots who feel they qualify—and don't. Most of the pilots will be well known, with a reputation to maintain.

2. One or two witnessed flights won't be enough to establish a Hang Four Rating, so some sort of log will probably be shown. The log entries covering the Hang Four requirements should have been signed by an observer. If there is no logbook, then it will be OK to have the segments signed off on the back of his Hang Three Rating card.

3. Entry Turns:
   a) These are 180-degree turns which are entered from a slight dive.
   b) A given *turn* rate is established and held.
   c) The airspeed is reduced at a constant rate throughout the turn so that, as the glider is rolled to level, at the 180-degree mark, the airspeed is approximately that of minimum sink.
   d) The bank angle should be smoothly reduced throughout the turn so that, as the airspeed drops, the turn rate is constant.
   e) No stall should be evident.
   f) The maneuver should be witnessed in both directions.
   g) The entire demonstration should leave no doubts in the mind of the observer.

4. 360-degree Turns: The following forms of the 360 must be witnessed:
   a) Basic 360:
      1) Left and right; gentle and steep.
      2) Precise pitch and lateral control must be witnessed. Just "banking and cranking" will not suffice.
   b) Entry turn so flown as to be a 360 instead of a 180. The turn should be entered from a crosswind leg so that the first portion is downwind.
   c) Entry turn that begins at minimum sink airspeed. Smoothly increase airspeed, maintaining maximum safe turning rate, so that at the 180-degree mark the airspeed is near the maximum L/D airspeed or slightly greater. Maintain this airspeed and maximum safe turning rate to completion. The roll-out should not exhibit marked pitch-up.
   d) Entry turn that must have at least maximum L/D airspeed to a medium bank. At the 90-degree mark, decisively roll to a maximum safe turn rate without pitching obviously up or down. Resume the original bank and turn rate at the 270-degree mark until completion of 360. Each demonstration will be to the left and right without noticeable slipping or skidding.

5. Turbulence: Controlled and unpanicked flight in conditions resulting in multiple sail inversions and requiring quick, deliberate, correct, and substantial control applications.

6. High Altitude:
   a) Flights in which terrain clearance exceeds at least 1,000 feet for at least three minutes.

    b) During such altitude conditions, 720-degree turns are accomplished in both directions.

    c) The pilot will have flown flights of over ten minutes.

    d) Balloon-launched flights over flat terrain are not to be used as evidence for this skill.

7. Cliff Launches:
    a) Cliffs to be precipitous and over 100 feet high.
    b) Launches must be either:
        1) Unassisted in near-calm conditions, or
        2) Assisted in windy conditions with strong lift right at takeoff.

8. Cross-country:
    a) Demonstrated ability to recognize landing areas previously visited on the ground but not visible at takeoff or during the first few minutes of flight.
    b) Must be able to determine wind direction from natural sources while in flight.
    c) Must be able to set up conservative planned approaches to strange landing areas allowing for surprises.
    d) Must be able to explain various means of determining possible locations of wires, fences, poles, etc.
    e) Must be able to discuss wind and lift in various regions such as canyons.
    f) Must be able to explain the correct use of airspeed in striving for maximum distance traveled over the ground in various conditions of wind and lift or sink.

9. Any requirement called for in lower Hang Ratings should be met by the pilot easily.

10. On the Hang Four card, there will be numbers representing the above skills. If they are not witnessed, they should be punched out with a hole punch.

HANG FIVE

This rating signifies that the pilot is capable of doing it all and that he knows enough to enter new conditions properly. He should have the freedom of any area without concern.

PILOT I.D.

Each rated pilot will, upon having been witnessed for a new level, receive a temporary receipt from the observer. The observer will retain a copy and send one to USHGA where a card will be made out and sent to the pilot. At intervals, the observer will be sent a list of these to check against his record. The special skills in the Hang Four will be treated as new ratings. The *Ground Skimmer* magazine will publish the higher ratings. Any false cards will result in the pilot's not being eligible for sanctioned contests, awards, and, probably, flying privileges at local sites. Again, it should be borne in mind that this program is not a licensing function. It is simply to make it possible for us all to go to various areas with a minimum of hassle.

Hang Gliding Directory

ON THE FOLLOWING pages you will find listings of hang gliding organizations, publications, manufacturers, dealers and flight schools. Compiled by the United States Hang Gliding Association (Box 66306, Los Angeles, California 90066, phone (213) 390-3065), they are up to date as of October 1974.

For greater convenience, listings are grouped by USHGA regions. Find your state in each subject category to look up information and find out about activities near you. Check other regions as well for more complete information.

ORGANIZATIONS

Northwest: Alaska, Idaho, Montana, Oregon, Washington

Inland Empire
c/o Bill Johnson
Box 2009
Missoula, MT 59801
(406) 549-5076

Oregon Hang Glider Assn.
Box 3815
Portland, OR 97208

Inland Empire Hang Gliders Assn.
Spokane, WA 99202

Pacific Northwest Hang Glider Assn., Inc.
c/o Vern Roundtree
30003-112 SE
Auburn, WA 98002

Robert Lockhart
604 N. 20 Ave.
Yakima, WA 98902

Eastern Washington Hang Gliding Assn.
c/o George Gregor
1425 Marshall
Richland, WA 99352

Northern California

Fellow Feathers
Self-Launched Pilots of San Francisco
2123 Junipero Serra Blvd.
Daly City, CA 94015

Wings of Rogallo
c/o Gary R. Warren
502 Barkentine Lane
Redwood City, CA 94065

Sierra Hang Gliding Assn.
c/o Bob Russell
Box 443
Sutter Creek, CA 95685

Southern California, Hawaii

United States Hang Gliding Assn., Inc.
Box 66306
Los Angeles, CA 90066
(213) 390-3065

Self-Soar Assn.
Box 1860
Santa Monica, CA 90406
(213) 395-4991

Ultralight Fliers Org.
Box 81665
San Diego, CA 92138

Orange County Sky Sailing
c/o Gail Montgomery
916 Delaware
Huntington Beach, CA 92648

Escape Country Sky Surfing Club
c/o Escape Country
Trabuco Canyon, CA 92678
(714) 586-7964

Kydid Flyer Club
323 N. Euclid, #140
Santa Ana, CA 92703

San Joaquin Valley Hang Gliding Club
1505 E. Magill
Fresno, CA 93710

Pacific Tradewind Skysailors, Ltd.
841 Bishop St., Suite 1401
Honolulu, HI 96813

Arizona, Colorado, Nevada, New Mexico, Utah, Wyoming

North American Sky Sailing Assn.
c/o Chandelle Corp.
15955-15 Ave.
Golden, CO 80401

Northern New Mexico Free Air Force
c/o G. A. Barber
Box 438
Chimayo, NM 87522
(505) 351-4894

Arkansas, Iowa, Kansas, Louisiana, Missouri, Nebraska, North Dakota, South Dakota, Oklahoma, Texas

Midwest Hang Glider Assn.
11959 Glenvalley Dr.
Maryland Heights, MO 63043
(314) 739-3456

North TX Hang Glider Society
1716 Jasmine Lane
Plano, TX 75014
424-1168

Hill Country Gliders
Rt. #1, Box 326
Wimberly, TX 78678

Illinois, Indiana, Michigan, Minnesota, Wisconsin

Ultralight Flight Organization of South eastern Mich.
2597 Kingstowne Dr.
Walled Lake, MI 48088

Northwestern Hang Gliders Assn.
212-15 Ave S
Minneapolis, MN 55404
(612) 894-2500

Wisconsin Self-Soaring
515 Milwaukee Ave.
S. Milwaukee, WI 53172
(414) 762-2751

Madison Sky Sailors
2925 Sachs St.
Madison, WI 53704
(608) 249-1669

Connecticut, Maine, Massachusetts, New Hampshire, Rhode Island, New York, Vermont

Connecticut Hang Gliders
c/o Bill Boyko, Pres.
27 Clear St.
Enfield, CT 06082
749-6340

Boston Sky Club
Box 375
Marlboro, MA 01752
(617) 485-5740

New England Hang Gliding
Box 356
Stoughton, MA 02072

Cole Hill Recreational, Inc.
Box 193 B
Berne, NY 12021
(518) 872-1820

Clarkson College Hang Glider Club
c/o Robert S. Murphy
Star Route
Potsdam, NY 13676

Hang Gliders of W. NY
c/o Paul Suozzi
2643 Union Rd.
Cheektowaga, NY 14227

Delaware, D. C., Kentucky, Maryland, New Jersey, Ohio, Pennsylvania, Virginia, West Virginia

Glide On Assn.
c/o T. S. Burnside, Pres.
323 Bradley Ave.
Rockville, MD 20851

Ohio Hang Glider Assn.
c/o Tony Mittelo
26875 Bagley Rd.
Berea, OH 44017

Capital Hang Glider Assn.
c/o Vic Powell
7358 Shenandoah Ave.
Annandale, VA 22003

Pittsburgh Hang Glider Assn.
Box 67
Trafford, PA 15085

Eastern Pennsylvania Hang Glider Assn.
620 Walnut St.
Reading, PA 19601

The Hang Glider Club of Virginia
c/o Davis Smith
1618 Jefferson Park #2A
Charlottesville, VA 22903

Tidewater Hang Glider Club
c/o Otto Horton, Jr.
5624 Hampshire Lane #102
Virginia Beach, VA 23462

Alabama, Florida, Georgia, Mississippi, North Carolina, Tennessee

North Carolina Hang Glider Soc.
c/o Tommy Thompson
104 Wright St.
Lewisville, NC 27023

Atlanta Ultralight Assoc.
c/o Dyches Boddiford
18 Peachtree Ave., #B-7
Atlanta, GA 30305

Canada

Alberta Hang Glider Assn.
2425-3 Ave. NW
Calgary, Alberta
Canada

Southern Ontario Hang Glider Assn.
c/o John D. Forman
10 Governors Rd.
Dundas, Ontario
Canada

PUBLICATIONS

Northwest: Alaska, Idaho, Montana, Oregon, Washington

OHGA Newsletter
Box 3815
Portland, OR 97208

Pacific NW Hang Glider Assn. Newsletter
c/o Vern Roundtree
30003-112 SE
Auburn, WA 98002

The Town Flyer
c/o Inland Empire Hang Gliders Assn.
Spokane, WA 99202

Northern California

Fellow Feathers Flash
2123 Junipero Serra Blvd.
Daly City, CA 94015

Wings of Rogallo Newsletter
502 Barkentine Lane
Redwood City, CA 94065

Southern California, Hawaii

Ground Skimmer
c/o USHGA, Inc.
Box 66306
Los Angeles, CA 90066

Kiting
3825½ Sawtelle
Los Angeles, CA 90066

Hang Glider Weekly
Box 1671
Santa Monica, CA 90406

Hang Glider Magazine
3333 Pacific Ave.
San Pedro, CA 90731

Delta Kite Flyer News
Box 483
Van Nuys, CA 91408

The Flier
Box 81665
San Diego, CA 92138

Skysailors Poopsheet
c/o Pacific Tradewinds Skysailors
841 Bishop St., Suite 1401
Honolulu, HI 96813

Arkansas, Iowa, Kansas, Louisiana, Missouri, Nebraska, North Dakota, South Dakota, Oklahoma, Texas

The Flatland Flyer
11959 Glenvalley Dr.
Maryland Heights, MO 63043
(314) 739-3456

Illinois, Indiana, Michigan, Minnesota, Wisconsin

Newsletter of the Ultralight Flight Org.
2597 Kingstowne Dr.
Walled Lake, MI 48088

Wind Free
c/o Madison Sky Sailors
2925 Sachs St.
Madison, WI 53704

Connecticut, Maine, Massachusetts, New Hampshire, Rhode Island, New York, Vermont

Newsletter, Ct. HGA
c/o Bill Boyko, Pres.
27 Clear St.
Enfield, CT 06082

Skysurfer
Box 375
Marlboro, MA 01752

The Ridge Rider
c/o New England Hang Gliding Assn.
Box 356
Stoughton, MA 02072

Delaware, D. C., Kentucky, Maryland, New Jersey, Ohio, Pennsylvania, Virginia, West Virginia

Ohio Hang Glider News Flyer
c/o Tony Mittelo
26875 Bagley Rd.
Berea, OH 44017

Skyline
Capital Hang Glider Assn.
7358 Shenandoah Ave.
Annandale, VA 22003

Alabama, Florida, Georgia, Mississippi, North Carolina, South Carolina, Tennessee

The Albatross
c/o Tommy Thompson
104 Wright St.
Lewisville, NC 27023

Canada

The Flypaper
Box 35, Site 13, RR 4
Calgary, Alberta
Canada

Up Draft
35 Mill St.
St. Albert, Alberta
Canada

MANUFACTURERS

Northwest: Alaska, Idaho, Montana, Oregon, Washington

Crown Enterprises
c/o Jerry Sanderson
40 E. Idaho St.
Kalispell, MT 59901
(406) 756-9377

Glider Sports International
2045 SE Hawthorne Blvd.
Portland, OR 97214

Beanway Flying Machines
Box 22524
Milwaukie, OR 97222
(503) 654-8530

Sailbird of Oregon
c/o David Miller
829 NE Imperial
Portland, OR 97232

Hang Ups, Inc.
30003-11 SE
Auburn, WA 98002
(206) 833-3003

Wings West
2608 NE 62
Seattle, WA 98115

Skysails, Inc.
1110 E. Pike
Seattle, WA 98122

Free Flight Dynamics
1915 Island View Pl.
Anacortes, WA 98221
(206) 293-7202

Northern California

Manta Products
1647 E. 14 St.
Oakland, CA 94606
(415) 536-1500

Ultralight Flying Machines
Box 59
Cupertino, CA 95014

True Flight
1719 Hillsdale Ave.
San Jose, CA 95142

Southern California, Hawaii

Dynasoar, Inc.
3518 Cahuenga Blvd.
W. Hollywood, CA 90068

Ultralite Products
137 Oregon St.
El Segundo, CA 90245
(213) 322-7171

Seagull Aircraft
3021 Airport Ave.
Santa Monica, CA 90405

Conquest Hang Gliders
323 Euclid N. #140
Santa Ana, CA 92703
(714) 554-0877

Glider Kites
13836 Cornuta
Bellflower, CA 90706

Eipper-Formance, Inc.
Box 246
Lomita, CA 90717
(213) 328-9100

Velderrain Hang Gliders
Box 314
Lomita, CA 90717
(213) 325-2960

Cliffhanger
Box 53
Paramount, CA 90723

Sunbird Ultralight Gliders
7219 Loma Verda Ave.
Canoga Park, CA 91303
(213) 882-3177

Sunbird Gliders
21420 Chase St., 7B
Canoga Park, CA 91304
(213) 882-3177

DSK Aircraft
11031 Glen Oaks Ave.
Pacoima, CA 91331

Free Flight Systems
12424 Gladstone Ave.
Sylmar, CA 91342
(213) 365-5607

The Bird People
Box 943
Sun Valley, CA 91352

Delta Wing Kites
Box 483
Van Nuys, CA 91408
(213) 785-2474

Hang Gliders of San Diego
4531 Mission Bay
San Diego, CA 92109

Hawk Industries
5111 Santa Fe St.
San Diego, CA 92109
(714) 272-7449

Volmer Aircraft
Box 5222
Glendale, CA 92201
(213) 247-8718

Solo Flight
930 W. Hoover Ave.
Orange, CA 92667
(714) 538-9768

Pacific Gull
1321 Calle Valle F
San Clemente, CA 92672

Sports Kites, Inc.
1202-C E. Walnut
Santa Ana, CA 92701
(714) 547-1344

Mehil Enterprises
5900 Canterbury
Culver City, CA 90230
(213) 648-3710

Hang Gliding Helmets
1331 Berea Pl.
Pacific Palisades, CA 90272

Sailrite Kits
2010 Lincoln Blvd.
Venice, CA 90291

Bird Feathers
1554-5 Ave.
Santa Monica, CA 90401

Supplies, Kits and Plans
5042 Malaga Dr.
La Palma, CA 90623

Wollard Products
(quick releases)
Box 268
Sunland, CA 91040
322-2509

Sky Craft
615 Ruberta Ave.
Glendale, CA 91201

Taras Kiceniuk, Jr.
(Icarus plans)
Palomar Observatory
Palomar, CA 92060

Frank Colver
(variometers)
3076 Roanoke Lane
Costa Mesa, CA 92626

Hall's Hawks
(Rogallo plans)
12561 Pearce St.
Garden Grove, CA 92643
(714) 455-6553

Windsong Hanglider Acc's.
27 N. Garden St.
Ventura, CA 93001

B W B Enterprises
(log books)
Box 5575
Inglewood, CA 93010

Kilbourne Sport Specialties
Box 8326
Stanford, CA 94305

Dunbar Sails
Grove St. Pier Bldg. A
Oakland, CA 94607

**Arizona, Colorado, Nevada,
New Mexico, Utah, Wyoming**

Sun Sail Corp.
6753 E. 47 Ave.
Denver, CO 80216
(303) 321-8482

Chandelle Corp.
15955-5 Ave.
Golden, CO 80401
(303) 278-9566

Sailbird Flying Machines
3123-A N. El Paso Rd.
Colorado Springs, CO 80907

Sky Bird Enterprises
4732 Bennett Dr.
Las Vegas, NV 89121

Sport Kites Albuquerque
Box 8382
Albuquerque, NM 87108

Kitty Hawk Hang Gliders & Ski Kites
3202 San Mateo NE
Albuquerque, NM 87110

Mountain Green Sailwing
Box 711
Morgan, UT 84050

Sport Kites Wyoming
Box 65
Shoshone, WY 82649

Sports Aloft, Inc.
Box 26
New Castle, WY 82701

**Arkansas, Iowa, Kansas, Louisiana,
Missouri, Nebraska, North Dakota,
Oklahoma, South Dakota, Texas**

Bede Development
Box 12128
Wichita, KS 67212

Pliable Moose Delta Wings
243 Matthewson
Wichita, KS 67214
(316) 262-2664

Kondor Kites
Box 603
Lewisville, TX 75067

Jack Hinson
5206 Greenville Ave.
Dallas, TX 75206

**Illinois, Indiana, Michigan, Minnesota,
Wisconsin**

Fire Craft, Inc.
c/o Dan Johnson
4904 N. Dalaski
Chicago, IL 60630

Dyna Soar Mfg. Co.
Box 236
Carmel, IN 46032

Marske Aircraft Corp.
130 Crestwood Dr.
Michigan City, IN 46360

Sport Wings, Inc.
Box 1647
Lafayette, IN 47902

Sky Sails of Michigan
1611 S. Woodward
Royal Oak, MI 48067
(313) 545-0051

Foot Launched Flyers
2597 Kingstowne Dr.
Walled Lake, MI 48088
(313) 285-6960

Icarus II
82 Fremont St.
Battle Creek, MI 49017

Delta Sail Wing Gliders
501 Westview Dr.
Hastings, MN 55038
(612) 437-2685

Aircraft Unlimited
Box 1616
Minneapolis Int'l. Airport
Minneapolis, MN 55111

Mike Flannigan
20560 Jamesville Rd.
Excelsior, MN 55331
(612) 474-3513

Delta Wing Kites
8620 W. Auer
Milwaukee, WI 53222
(414) 442-9152

Aspen Enterprises
Box 423
Neenah, WI 54946

Connecticut, Maine, Massachusetts, New Hampshire, Rhode Island, New York, Vermont

Sky Sports, Inc.
Ellington Airport
Ellington, CT 06029

Zepher Aircraft Corp.
25 Mill St.
Glastonbury, CT 06033
(203) 633-9074

Man Flight Systems, Inc.
Box 375
Marlboro, MA 01752

New York Hang Gliders, Inc.
144-45 35 Ave.
Flushing, NY 11354
(212) 762-1280

Dixson Hang Glider Supplies & School
5 Arden Lane
Farmingville, NY 11738
(516) 588-7562

Delaware, D. C., Kentucky, Maryland, New Jersey, Ohio, Pennsylvania, Virginia, West Virginia

Deltasoarus, Inc.
131 Bound Brook Rd.
Parsippany, NJ 07054

Chuck's Glider Supplies
4200 Royalton Rd.
Brecksville, OH 44141
(216) 236-8440

Kitty Hawk Kites
308 Gilpin Ave.
Norfolk, VA 23503
(804) 588-4223

Alabama, Florida, Georgia, Mississippi, North Carolina, South Carolina, Tennessee

Sail Bird Flying Machines
6309 S. Adelia Ave.
Tampa, FL 33616

Johnson Flex-Wing Kites
Box 91
Cypress Gardens, FL 33880

WDM Enterprises
2770 Bufordi Dr.
Marietta, GA 30060

Flight Dynamics, Inc.
Box 5070
Raleigh, NC 27607

Cloudman Glidercraft Co.
905 Church St.
Nashville, TN 37203

Wings Aloft
6232 Vance Rd.
Chattanooga, TN 37421

Butterfly Ind., Inc.
1911 W. Cumberland Ave.
Knoxville, TN 37916

Canada

Birdman Enterprises
8011 Argyll Rd.
Edmonton, Alberta
Canada

B & T Enterprises
Box 1874
Calgary, Alberta
Canada, T2P 2L8

The Werner Kausche Co. & Work Shc
215-11 Ave. SW
Calgary, Alberta
Canada

Muller Kites LTD
Box 4063 Postal St. C
Calgary, Alberta
Canada T2T 5M9

Sky and Earth Systems
81 Huntingwood Cres.
Bramalea, Ontario
Canada

Europe, Africa

Manufacture De Cerfs-Volants
2/30 Sq. Hector Berlioz
94700 Malsons-Alfort
France

South African Aviation Centre
Box 33191, Jeppestown, Transvaal
Burco Hs, 17 Error St.
New Doornfont
Johannesburg, South Africa

DEALERS AND SCHOOLS

Northwest: Alaska, Idaho, Montana, Oregon, Washington

Klean Fun Kites
Box 4-2990
Anchorage, AK 99503

Gary King, Jr.
308 E. Northern Lights Blvd.
Anchorage, AK 99503

Falcon Air
4049 Mallard
Fairbanks, AK 99701

Upward Bound South
1110 N. 2 Ave.
Pocatello, ID 83201
(208) 233-8127

Free Flight of Twin Falls
259 Main Ave. E.
Twin Falls, ID 83301

Sun Valley Kite School
Box 1077
Ketchum, ID 83340

Chandelle of Idaho
Box 1221
Sun Valley, ID 83353

Sun Valley Kite School
Box 243
Sun Valley, ID 83353
(208) 622-3511

Soaring Sports
Box 2764
Idaho Falls, ID 83501
(208) 523-1677

Free Flight of Caldwell
Rt. #3
Caldwell, ID 83605

Jones Brothers
2901 State St.
Boise, ID 83702
(208) 344-7774

Mike Hester
3051 Rowland Lane
Boise, ID 83703

Millers Marina & Pro-shop
1710 S. Roosevelt St.
Boise, ID 83705
(208) 343-2830

Pegasus Aeronautics
636-5 Ave.
Lewiston, ID 85501
(208) 743-8341

Free Flight of Moorhead
The Escape Hatch
1815 N. 11 St.
Moorhead, MT 56560

Free Flight of Montana
221 Jackson St.
Billings, MT 59101
248-6717

George V. Nilson, NFT Inc.
Box 2367
Great Falls, MT 59103
(406) 453-5183

Free Flight of Poplar
Box 35
Poplar, MT 59255

Free Flight of Helena
718 Broadway
Helena, MT 59601

Big Sky Delta Wing Kites
201 E. Central
Missoula, MT 59801

Upward Bound
Box 2009
Missoula, MT 59801
(406) 549-5076

Cyngus Sky School
Box 244
Rhododendron, OR 97049

Delta Wing Gliders of Mt. Hood
2604 NE 61 Ave.
Portland, OR 97213
(503) 281-1484

Hang Gliders Northwest
c/o John Ford
312 NE 84 St.
Portland, OR 97220
(503) 253-6631

Free Flight of Oregon
Box N
Corvallis, OR 97330
(503) 752-9036

Pacific Hang Gliders
1729 Labona Dr.
Eugene, OR 97401
(503) 484-9900

Rex Miller
634-A E. 8 Ave.
Eugene, OR 97403

Nest Airplane Works
1445½ W. 11 Ave.
Eugene, OR 97402

Oregon Manta
350 W. 4 Ave.
Eugene, OR 97403

Southern Oregon Marina
Box 37
Phoenix, OR 97535
(503) 535-2396

C & D Sports
Box 52
Baker, OR 97814
(503) 523-5183

Cascade Free Flight
Box 176
Duvall, WA 98010
(206) 788-1002

Pacific Northwest Hang Gliding Scho
10831 NE 112 Ave.
Kirkland, WA 98033

Chandelle Northwest
77 Madison St.
Seattle, WA 98104
(206) 682-4655

H & H Water Sports, Inc.
1006 S. 198 Pl.
Seattle, WA 98148
(206) 824-2668

Bruce Barr
17360 Beach Dr. NE
Seattle, WA 98155
(206) 363-0900

J Bird Hang Gliders
Rt. #5, Box 234-A, SP #2
Arlington, WA 98223

Fairhaven Kite Co.
1200 Harris St.
Bellingham, WA 98225

Delta Wing Kites, Inc.
20928-133 St. SE
Monroe, WA 98272
(206) 794-6540

Hang In There Baby
c/o Derco
Box 11
Keyport, WA 98345

Cliffhanger Kite Co.
c/o Wendell Litke
3009 N. McCarver
Tacoma, WA 98403

Jerry Bain
309 N. 19 St.
Kelso, WA 98626
(206) 425-5211

Delta Wing Kites
1700 Washington Bldg.
Seattle, WA 98101

Sport Kites Spokane
c/o Bob Bird
Box 7400
Spokane, WA 99207

Pegasus Aeronautics
N. 4914 Ash
Spokane, WA 99208
(509) 328-3797

George Gregor
1425 Marshall
Richland, WA 99325
(509) 943-3951

Ben Franklin's Kite Shop
11430 SE Reedway
Portland, OR 97266
(503) 771-3147

Northern California

Don Partridge
Box 404
Bishop, CA 93514
(714) 873-5070

Jim Green
3726 N. Van Ness Blvd.
Fresno, CA 93704
(209) 222-6025

Tic Musser
2842 N. Hacienda
Fresno, CA 93705
(209) 227-2282

Chandelle Fresno
c/o Alpine Shop
4777 Blackstone
Fresno, CA 93726
(209) 299-9591

Monarch Skysails
136 E. Olive
Fresno, CA 93728

Free Flight of the Monterey Peninsula
2201 Fremont Blvd.
Monterey, CA 93904

Seagull Soaring
Box 5474
Carmel, CA 93921
(408) 394-3347

J. L. Enterprises
Box 802
Belmont, CA 94002

Falcon Hang Gliding
1121 Burlingame Ave.
Burlingame, CA 94010
(415) 342-2210

Chandelle San Francisco
2123 Junipero Serra Blvd.
Daly City, CA 94015
(415) 756-0650

Fellow Feathers
Self-Launched Pilots of San Francisco
2123 Junipero Serra Blvd.
Daly City, CA 94015

Volbron Hang Glider School
2465 Bantry Lane
S. San Francisco, CA 94080
(415) 873-1731

J & G Aircraft
1137 Jameston Dr.
Sunnyvale, CA 94087
(415) 948-4524

Come Fly a Kite
900 North Point
San Francisco, CA 94109

Free Flight of Fresno
Box 589
Fresno, CA 94509

Manta Livermore
2582-1 St.
Livermore, CA 94550
(415) 477-7100

Sport Kites Pleasanton
c/o Tom Drengacz
1642 Harvest Rd.
Pleasanton, CA 94566

Phantom Wing, Inc.
43 Panoramic Way
Walnut Creek, CA 94595

Eagle Wings, Inc.
2627 Berkeley
Berkeley, CA 94704

Northern California Sun
Box 1624
Sausalito, CA 94965
(415) 388-2923

Boat & Motor Mart
3250 Army St.
San Francisco, CA 94110
(415) 824-3545

Angle Wing Kite Sales & Ground Scho
236 Santa Cruz Ave.
Aptos, CA 95003
(408) 688-3045

Aeolus Hang Gliders
529 Capitola Ave.
Capitola, CA 95010

Aeolus Hang Gliders
631 Redwood Rd.
Felton, CA 95018
(408) 335-5798

Free Flight of Stockton
1135 Delivery
Stockton, CA 95204

Bill Johnson
2211 Vera Cruz
Modesto, CA 95350
(207) 521-5289

Free Flight of Manteca
17810 Kram
Manteca, CA 95366

Bruce Shade
4817 Forrestal St.
Fair Oaks, CA 95628
(916) 961-1472

Ron Rupp
Homewood Resort, Box 165
Homewood, CA 95718
(916) 525-7256

Tahoe Hang Glider Specialist
Box 2366
Olympic Valley, CA 95730
(916) 582-2700

Sacramento Valley Hang Gliders
3210 Balmoral Dr.
Sacramento, CA 95821
(916) 489-0476

Free Flight of Chico
c/o Charles Funk and Cecil Hall
848 W. 9
Chico, CA 95926

Sail Wing Sky School North
2631-A Rancho Rd.
Redding, CA 96001

Southern California, Hawaii

Flex-O-Kite Ski Co.
13618 Catalina Ave.
Gardena, CA 90247

Sail Wing, Inc., School
1116-8 St.
Manhattan Beach, CA 90266

West Wind School of Hang Gliding
Box 331
Manhattan Beach, CA 90266

Astro Flight, Inc.
13377 Beach Ave.
Venice, CA 90291

Air Supply
2230 Michigan Ave.
Santa Monica, CA 90404

Soaring Emporium
20123 Hawthorne Blvd.
Torrance, CA 90503
(213) 371-6130

Condor Kites
5507 Calle Mayor
Torrance, CA 90505

P R N Systems
6580 Capers Way
Cypress, CA 90630

The Hang Glider Shop
1351 S. Beach Ave.
La Habra, CA 90631

Bob Velzy
13077 E. Rosecrans Blvd.
Santa Fe Springs, CA 90670
(213) 921-4111

Aerodyne Co.
9460 Artesia Blvd.
Bellflower, CA 90706

Aero Crafts
Box 8175A
La Crescenta, CA 91214

Free Flight Systems
Hang Gliding School
12424 Gladstone Ave.
Sylmar, CA 91242

Delta Ray Kites
16603 Covello St.
Van Nuys, CA 91406

Delta Wing Flight School
Box 483
Van Nuys, CA 91408
(213) 785-2474

Windways Flying Machines
1368 Max Ave.
Chula Vista, CA 92011
(714) 427-8514

Daedalus
111-12 St.
Del Mar, CA 92014

Keen Things Enterprises
1064 Merritt Dr.
El Cajon, CA 92020
(714) 447-5923

Skylark Gliders
1867 Candle Lane
El Cajon, CA 92020

Pacific Ultralight
c/o Dous Fronius
100 Stoney Knoll Rd.
El Cajon, CA 92021

Livesay Mfg.
9489 Mission Park Pl.
Santee, CA 92071
(714) 449-0343

Natural Flight Systems
Box 7374
San Diego, CA 92107

Sure Flight School
c/o Ralph Chaney
4575 Caper Way
San Diego, CA 92107

Hang Gliders of San Diego
163 Turquoise St.
San Diego, CA 92109
(714) 488-3175

Jim Rusing
Sea World
1720 S. Shores Rd.
San Diego, CA 92109
(714) 222-6363 ext. 216

Westerly Sails
c/o Dale Braegger
3912 W. Pt. Loma Blvd.
San Diego, CA 92115

Hang Craft of San Diego
317 Dewey St.
San Diego, CA 92113

Feather Sky Sails
Box 0172
San Diego, CA 92115

Free Flight of San Diego
Box 15722
San Diego, CA 92115

Flight Realities
1945-C Adams Ave.
San Diego, CA 92116
(714) 298-1962

Albatross Sails
11545 Sorrento Valley Rd.
San Diego, CA 92121

Hang Gliders of Calif.
11545 Sorrento Valley Rd.
Bldg. 3, Suite 303
San Diego, CA 92121
(714) 452-0351

Fly Me Kites
Box 444-4
Running Springs, CA 92382

Hang Gliders
24523 Monterey
San Bernadino, CA 92410

Free Flight of Orange
Box 485
Costa Mesa, CA 92627
(714) 642-5656

Fly High Sails
12702 Lorna St. #B
Garden Grove, CA 92641

Speed & Marine Assoc.
401 W. Chapman
Orange, CA 92666

Solo Flight, Inc.
930 W. Hoover Ave.
Orange, CA 92667

Chuck Stahl
26671 La Sierra
Mission Viejo, CA 92627
(714) 831-1861

Escape Country
Attn: Hang Gliding School
Robinson Ranch
Trabuco Canyon, CA 92678
(714) 586-7964

Chandelle West Hang Gliding School
17815-A Sky Park
Irvine, CA 92707
(714) 979-7413

Sky King Enterprises
1101 W. Stevens #47
Santa Ana, CA 92707

Windsong Hang Gliding School
27 N. Garden
Ventura, CA 93001

Free Flight of Ventura
Ultra Light Hang Gliders
Box 2094
Ventura, CA 93001
(805) 648-6687

Casa De Motor Homes
2605 Wagon Wheel Dr.
Oxnard, CA 93030
(805) 485-1818

Free Flight of Santa Barbara
1806-J Cliff Dr.
Santa Barbara, CA 93105

Flight Realities
2414 Park Way
Bakersfield, CA 93304
(805) 323-9759

Ray Shannon
512 Jefferson
Bakersfield, CA 93305
(805) 327-2054

William Wooley, Jr.
3801 Allen Rd.
Bakersfield, CA 93307
(805) 589-2555

Full Wing Flight School
Box 893
Morro Bay, CA 93442

David Rachubka
3121 Coral St.
Morro Bay, CA 93442
(805) 772-3794

Aero Specialties Co.
1205 W. Main St.
Santa Maria, CA 93454

Sport Kites Kauai
c/o John Hughes
Box 337
Lawai, Kauai, HI 96765

Dick Eipper
Box 244
Kula, Maui, HI 96790

Stan Truett
Box 7
Kula, Maui, HI 96790

Sport Kites Oahu
c/o Mike Dorn
5283 Kalantianaole Hwy.
Honolulu, HI 96812

Air Performance Hawaii
217 Prospect
Honolulu, HI 96813

Manta Hawaii
726 S. Queen St.
Honolulu, HI 96813

Ultralight Flying Mach.
c/o Dave Bettencourt
841 Bishop St., Suite 1401
Honolulu, HI 96813

Dove Hang Gliders of Hawaii
2445 Ala Wai #5
Honolulu, HI 96815

O'Brien Kites
c/o Larry D. Smith
1637 Kapiolani Blvd.
Honolulu, HI 96816

**Arizona, Colorado, Nevada,
New Mexico, Utah, Wyoming**

Chandelle Phoenix
Ski Haus Action Sports
2501 E. Indian School Rd.
Phoenix, AZ 85016

U.S. Hang Gliders
11024 N. 22 Ave. #5
Phoenix, AZ 85016

John Fox
3147 N. 31 Ave.
Phoenix, AZ 85017
(602) 272-6661

Genesis II, Inc.
Box 3526
Phoenix, AZ 85030

Sport-Air
4313 E. University
Phoenix, AZ 85040

Jim Allen
6016 E. Quartz Mt. Rd.
Paradise, AZ 85253
(602) 948-0734

Bill Allen
2638 N. Champlain
Temple, AZ 85281
(602) 945-2514

Free Flight of Az.
Star Rt., Box 5
Winkelman, AZ 85292

Chandelle Tucson
Ski Haus Action Sports
2823 E. Speedway
Tucson, AZ 85705

Icarus II
2762 N. Stone
Tucson, AZ 85705

Hang Gliders, Inc.
1300 E. Valencia
Tucson, AZ 85706

Hi Country Bicycle Works
701 W. Hampden Ave.
Cinderella City
Englewood, CO 80110
(303) 761-6113

Alpine Haus
1600-8 Ave.
Greenley, CO 80221

Rocky Mountain Marine
5411 Leetsdale Dr.
Denver, CO 80222

Manta Midwest
765 Noble St.
Golden, CO 80401

Summit Flight
Breckenridge, CO 80424

C. B. Jensen Group
c/o JLS Flying Service
Box 22
Hideaway Park, CO 80450
(303) 726-5969

Naturally High Flight Systems
Box 5218
Steamboat, CO 80477

Alpine Haus
628 S. College
Fort Collins, CO 80521

Free Flight of Canon City
Fremont Sales & Service
Box 70
Canon City, CO 81212

Free Flight of Alamosa
3 Bellwood Dr.
Alamosa, CO 81101

Get High, Inc.
Box 4451
Aspen, CO 81611
(303) 925-3275

Gorsuch, Ltd.
Box 1508
Vail, CO 81657
(303) 925-3275

Life Cycle
1224-15 St.
Denver, CO 82020
(303) 572-0405

Wings, c/o Bill Duca
906 S. 4 St.
Las Vegas, NV 89101
(702) 384-3458

Sierra Wings
890 E. Main St.
Falon, NV 89406

Sierra Hang Glider School
Box 4557
Stateline, NV 89449
(702) 583-3910

Sierra Wings
253 E. Arroyo
Reno, NV 89502

New Mexico Ski Sails
635 Amherst NE
Albuquerque, NM 87106

Sky Sailors Sales & Service
7280 Arroyo Del Oro, NE
Albuquerque, NM 87109

New Mexico Hang Gliding School
1825 Mary Ellen NE #1
Albuquerque, NM 87112

Base Camp
121 W. San Francisco St.
Santa Fe, NM 87501
(505) 982-9707

Danny King
Box 877
Deming, NM 88030
(505) 546-5738

Chandelle Utah/Sky School
3698 E. 7000 S.
Salt Lake City, UT 84017
(801) 277-3944

Free Flight of Salt Lake City
6073 S. 530 W.
Murray, UT 84017

Delta Ray Kites
1704 N. Valley View Dr.
Layton, UT 84041

Larry Matson Hang Gliding School
1507 S. 1600 E.
Salt Lake City, UT 84105

Tom Vadaya
3209 Imperial St.
Salt Lake City, UT 84106

Miller Ski & Cycle Haus
834 Washington Blvd.
Ogden, UT 84401
(801) 392-3911

Sunset Sport Center
2909 Washington Blvd.
Odgen, UT 84401
(801) 487-3586

Robertson Marine
97 S. Main St.
Springville, UT 84663

Alpine Haus
111 W. 17
Cheyenne, WY 82001

Sailbird of Utah
847 N. 750 E.
Layton, UT 84041

Alpine Haus
17 and Grand Ave.
Laramie, WY 82070

Snow King Ski School
Box R
Jackson, WY 83001

Arkansas, Iowa, Kansas, Louisiana, Missouri, Nebraska, North Dakota, Oklahoma, South Dakota, Texas

Stanley Newton
Box 163, Rt. #5
Hot Springs, AR 71901

Stanley E. Samuelson
Osceola, IA 50213
(515) 342-2789

Boag Chumbley
8219 Lista Lane & 1323 Park Ave.
Des Moines, IA 50315
(515) 285-8594

Peter Hadley
6901 W. 194
Stillwell, KS 66085
(913) 432-4766

D. W. Kites Sales & Service
200 W. 30, STE #102
Topeka, KS 66611

Mid West Wings
202 S. Fourth
Osborne, KS 67473

Wills Wing Training School
Michael S. Laakko
308 E. Pine #3
Wichita, KS 67214

Benny Jumper
Country Estates 12B
Kays, KS 67601
(913) 625-7576

Charles Elmer
7902 Breakwater Dr.
New Orleans, LA 70124
(504) 885-0449

Ark-La-Tek Divers Supply
9118 Blom
Shreveport, LA 71108

Hunts Kites
Al Signonini
11959 Glenvalley Dr.
Maryland Heights, MO 63043
(314) 739-3456

Ray Wall's Delta Wing Kites
Rt. #1
Wappapello Lake, MO 63966

Kitty Hawk
230 W. McDaniel
Springfield, MO 65806
866-4501

City Lock & Marine
2031 St. Mary's Ave.
Omaha, NE 68102
(402) 341-9672

Buzz's Body Shop & Marine Supply
RR Ave. E, Box 72
Kearney, NE 68847
(402) 237-2624

Midwest Free Flight
Box 205
Fairfield, NE 68938

John F. Rademacher
101-2 St. S.
Fargo, ND 58102

South Central Kite & Glider Enterprises
5206 Greenville Ave.
Dallas, TX 75206

Sky Sails, Inc.
3432 Dalworth
Arlington, TX 76011
(817) 261-3462

Free Flight of Temple
American Handicrafts
719 S. 25 St.
Temple, TX 76501

Laudar Aerial
c/o John Tyson
2120 S. Post Oak Rd. #6
Houston, TX 77027
(713) 627-3613

Houston Delta Wing
c/o George P. Lasko, Jr.
10614 Plainfield
Houston, TX 77071
(714) 772-8619

Steven L. Branson
8718 Dale Valley
San Antonio, TX 78228
(512) 675-0786

Free Flight of Corpus Christi
Dockside, 315 Beach St.
Box 772
Port Arkansas, TX 78373
(512) 749-6141

David O'Neal
2118-70
Lubbock, TX 79412
(806) 744-2121

Illinois, Indiana, Michigan, Minnesota, Wisconsin

Chandelle Chicago
109 W. Prospect
Mt. Prospect, IL 60056
(312) 398-3451

Sailbird of Chicago
John Prescott
305 S. Wright
Naperville, IL 60540

Free Flight of Indianapolis
Box 297
Fishers, IN 46060

Hoosier Hang Gliders
c/o Greg Rector
707 Highwood
Greencastle, IN 46315

Chandelle Sky Sails of Michigan
c/o Adco, Inc.
30233 Southfield
Southfield, MI 48076

Manta Michigan
756 Hanley Dr.
Birmingham, MI 48080

Eco-Flight Systems, Inc.
2275 S. State
Ann Arbor, MI 48104
(313) 994-9020

Free Flight of Ann Arbor
8778 Main St.
Whitmore Lake, MI 48189

Free Flight of Detroit
19366 Kelly Rd.
Harper Woods, MI 48225

Great Lakes Sky Sails
5125 N. River Rd.
Freeland, MI 48623
(517) 695-5607

Great Lakes Sky Sails
837 E. Grand River Ave.
E. Lansing, MI 48906
(517) 351-1325

Sky Hook Sails of West Michigan
428 Ranney St.
Kalamazoo, MI 49001

AA Flight Systems
102 W. Buffalo
New Buffalo, MI 49117

Felix Marine
14023 Green
Grand Haven, MI 49417
(616) 842-3680

Chandelle of West Michigan
25 W. 9 St.
Holland, MI 49423

Skyscape Sports
25 W. 9 St.
Holland, MI 49423

D & D Skysailing
987 Fennwood
N. Muskegon, MI 49445
744-4288

Delta Wing of Mich.
1434 Lake Dr. SE
Grand Rapids, MI 49506

Gar's Sports Center
c/o Gary J. Meernik
2531 S. Division Ave.
Grand Rapids, MI 49507

Sugarloaf Sky School
RR #1
Cedar, MI 49621

Michigan Manta
c/o David Nelson
327 Main St., Box 70
Frankfort, MI 49635

Chandelle
RR #3, State Rd.
Harbor Springs, MI 49740

Dave Tiemeyer
Star Rt. 550, Box 334
Marquette, MI 49855

Free Flight of St. Paul
c/o Norcat Co.
2210 Whitebear
Maplewood, MN 55109

H. H. Petrie's Sporting Goods
Box 5427
Madison, WI 53703
(608) 256-1347

Delta Sports
3325 Park Ave. S.
Madison, WI 53705

Northwestern Hang Gliders Inc.
1215 Washington Ave. S.
Minneapolis, MN 55404
(612) 341-3322

Midwest Hanggliders
2002 Garfield Ave. S. #24
Minneapolis, MN 55408
(612)'874-9868

Alpine Imports Ltd.
Box 97
Crystal Lake, IL 60014
(815) 459-1816

Apollo Skysailing Centers
722 Barrington Rd.
Streamwood, IL 60103
(312) 289-5313

Arthur R. Koch
9702 Shore Dr.
Rockford, IL 61111
(815) 654-0080

Harold W. Lewis
139 S. Center St.
E. Alton, IL 62024
(618) 259-4737

Ben Heck
7191 W. Grand
Chicago, IL 60635
(312) 637-1007

Thomas Drewek
27073 Bonnie Dr.
Warren, MI 48093

Rudolph Kishazy
1460 Junction #3
Plymouth, MI 48170
(313) 455-7920

Munson Marine, Inc.
Box 538, RFD 1
Round Lake, IL 60073
(815) 358-2720

Jim Laure
1441 Spruce Dr.
Kalamazoo, MI 49001
(616) 327-3075

Easy Traveling Corp.
426 S. Burdick St.
Kalamazoo, MI 49006
(616) 343-1480

Prime Time Products, Inc.
Box 244
Sarmac, MI 48881

Free Flight of Watertown
857 Silver Lake St.
Oconomowoc, WI 53066

Tommy Bartlett Water Shows
Box 65
Wisconsin Dells, WI 53965
(608) 253-3031

Custom Displays
1530 Monroe Ave., NW
Grand Rapids, MI 49505
(616) 364-4510

Mornes, Inc.
1022 W. 4 St.
Grand Rapids, MN 55744

Arrow Marine
Hwy. 14 W. & 7 St. NW
Rochester, MN 55901

Fred Tiemens
1215 Washington Ave. S.
Minneapolis, MN 55404

Midwest Sports Center
Fairmont, MN 56031

**Connecticut, Maine, Massachusetts,
New Hampshire, Rhode Island,
New York, Vermont**
───────────────────────────────

Connecticut Hang Glider Assn.
58 Gail Rd.
E. Hartford, CT 06108

Lee Keeler
Purchase Hill
Southbury, CT 06488
(203) 354-7231

Aero Glide Airfoil, Inc.
Box 4108
Hamden, CT 06514

Adventurer Hang Gliders
Box 518
Loring AFB
Limestone, ME 04750

Patrick Mouligne
Sugarloaf Ski School
Sugarloaf, ME 04947

Sky Trukin', Inc.
Box 142
Kingfield, ME 04947

Free Flight of Maine
Snoop Sales
63 Union St.
Bangor, ME 08401

Brodie Mt. Kite School
c/o Brodie Mt. Ski Area, Rt. 7
New Ashford, MA 01237
(413) 443-4752

Paul Laliberte
Star Route
Kingsfield, ME 04947

Niemi Manufacturing Co.
25 Willow St.
Fitchburg, MA 01420
(617) 345-7337

Man Flight Systems, Inc.
Box 872
Worchester, MA 01613

Manta East
1 Veteran Rd.
Woburn, MA 01801
(617) 935-6127

Pliable Moose Delta Sky Sails of Wichita, K
17 Norfolk St.
Haverhill, MA 01841
(617) 372-6601

Sky Sports, Inc.
542 E. Squantum St.
North Quincy, MA 02171
(617) 328-0800

Strong Enterprises
542 E. Squantum Way
North Quincy, MA 02171

Dana L. Littlefield
97 Piney Point Dr.
Centerville, MA 02632

Terry Sweeney
RFD #2
Concord, NH 03301
(603) 774-4700

Fuji Industries Corp.
26 Broadway
New York, NY 10004
(212) 943-4435

Go Fly A Kite
1613-2 St.
New York, NY 10028
(212) 988-8885

Dixon's Hang Gliders & Supplies
5 Arden Lane
Farmingville, NY 11738
(516) 588-7562

Free Flight of Hicksville
77 E. End Ave.
Hicksville, Long Island
NY 11801

Long Island Kite Distributors
5 Bethpage Rd.
Hicksville, NY 11801
(516) 681-8738

The Hang Glider Store
Box 7, Ridge Rd.
Marlboro, NY 12542

Phoenicia Ultralight Flight Center
c/o The Hang Glider Store
Box 57, Ridge Rd.
Marlboro, NY 12542

Chandelle Birch Hill, Inc.
Box 283
Patterson, NY 12563

Arturo Lebron Flying Mach.
Division Lebron-Krawec
Box 119
Mountaindale, NY 12763

Windworld
401 Breakspear Rd.
Syracuse, NY 13219

Free Flight of Fayetteville
Hoag Lane
Fayetteville, NY 13615
(315) 341-5062

Free Flight of New York
c/o Mark J. Senit
Herkimer, NY 13350

David Montrois
Box 441
Brownsville, NY 13615
(315) 341-5062

Tim Eldridge
Box 42
Oneonta, NY 13820
(607) 432-4435

Dick Reynolds
RD 1, Uppereast St.
Oneonta, NY 13820
(607) 432-5418

Hang Gliders of W. NY
Box 219
East Aurora, NY 14052

Free Flight of Buffalo, Inc.
3973 Harlem Rd.
Amherst, NY 14226

Zepher Aircraft
c/o Bill Tucher
RD 3, Old Buffalo Rd.
Warsaw, NY 14569

Southern Tier Flight Shop
Rt. 99, Osceola Rd.
Woodhull, NY 14898

Trac & Trail Supply, Inc.
Rt. 107
Gaysville, VT 05746
(802) 234-9684

Delaware, D. C., Kentucky, Maryland, New Jersey, Ohio, Pennsylvania, Virginia, West Virginia

East Coast Hang Gliders
Box 961
Washington, DC 20044

Ron Oakley
8400 Blue Lick Rd.
Louisville, KY 40219
(502) 969-6295

Buel Stalls, Jr.
Box 69
Murray, KY 42071
(502) 753-3474

Chandelle Maryland
5603 McKinley
Bethesda, MD 20034

Sport Flight
3305 Ferndale St.
Kensington, MD 20795

Gill Enterprises
79 Herrington Dr.
Upper Marlboro, MD 20870

Ferranti's Phoenix Hang Glider Co.
128 Severn Ave.
Annapolis, MD 21403

James M. Krauk
8023 Yellowstone Rd.
Kingsville, MD 21087
(301) 592-2233

Jeffair
1107 Primrose Ct. #30
Annapolis, MD 21403

Bennett Delta Kites Gliders—East
Box 74
Holmdel, NJ 07054
(201) 542-8535

Lighter Than Air Products
40 Center St.
Springfield, NJ 07081
(201) 467-3562

Joe Mirnov
876 Red Rd.
Teaneck, NJ 07666
(201) 836-9210

Free Flight of Lebanon
1 Lynwood Dr.
Lebanon, NJ 08833

Action Sport Cycles
108 Essex Ave.
Metuchen, NJ 08840
(201) 494-5555

Ohio Hang Glider Assn.
c/o Tony Mittelo
26875 Bagley
Berea, OH 44017

Recreational Flying Machines
Airport Rd. Rt. 3
Saint Clairsville, OH 43950

Troyer Kite Supply
4299 Kent Rd.
Stow, OH 44224

Donald Boor
60 Woodland Ave.
Masury, OH 44438

Free Flight of Mansfield
2429 Panonia Rd.
Mansfield, OH 44903

Ross Strayer
742 Park View Dr.
Wauseon, OH 43567

Pennsylvania Sport Kites
c/o Richard Wilson
6052 Dalmatian Dr.
Bethel Park, PA 15102

Free Flight of Greensburg
Log Cabin Wholesale Tire, RD 1
Greensburg, PA 15601
523-3788

Icarus, Inc.
221 Allen St.
State College, PA 16801

Lancaster County Marine
Rt. 222, 4 Lauber Rd.
Akron, PA 17501
(717) 859-1121

Icarus, Inc.
Box 51
Broomall, PA 19008

Free Flight of Eastern Penn.
620 Walnut St.
Reading, PA 19601

The Kite Exchange
7358 Shenandoah Ave.
Annondale, VA 22003

Max Tufts, Jr.
Box 166
Warrenton, VA 22186
(703) 347-1376

Dave Gibson
823 Pepper Ave.
Richmond, VA 23226
(804) 285-4095

Delta Wing Kites
c/o Larry Davis
Rt. 6, Box 94
Martinsville, VA 24112

Frederic A. Munson
Smith Mountain Dock, Inc.
Penhook, VA 24137
(703) 927-5100

J. J. Skysurfing, Inc.
c/o John Sleely, Jr.
Box 1181
Martinsburg, WVA 25401

**Alabama, Florida, Georgia, Mississippi,
North Carolina, South Carolina, Tennessee**

Jerry H. Blount
804 Poinciana Dr.
Gulf Breeze, FL 32561
(904) 932-4138

Jerry Hogan
360 S. Highway 19
Crystal River, FL 32629
(904) 795-4736

Island Park Bayfront
Box 2868
Sarasota, FL 32629
(813) 366-6659

Freeform, Inc.
1201 N. Highland Ave.
Clearwater, FL 33515

Hal Elgin's Holiday Water Sports
6639 Emerson Ave. S
Petersburgh, FL 33707
(813) 345-3697

Jim McCormick Ski School
Box 84
Cypress Gardens, FL 33880

B & H Sales
349 N. Four Lane Highway
Marietta, GA 30060
(404) 428-0037

Larry Helmer
860 Lindberg
Atlanta, GA 30324

Appalachian Mountaineering
5725 Buford Highway, NE
Atlanta, GA 30340

Jimmy Spears
128 Reynolds St.
Augusta, GA 30901
(401) 738-7415

R. B. Prichard
330 Foster Park
Bonneville, MS 38829
(601) 728-5957

Doss & Sons
434 Brookstown Ave.
Winston-Salem, NC 27101

Free Flight of Greensboro
c/o Frank J. Howard
2300 Phoenix Dr.
Greensboro, NC 27406

Kitty Hawk Kites
Box 386
Nags Head, NC 27959
(919) 441-6247

Land, Air and Sea Venture
Box 275
Wrightsville Beach, NC 28480

Patton Motor Homes, Inc.
4809 Wilkinson Blvd.
Charlotte, NC 29208

J & P Distributors
Box 278
Lebanon, TN 37087

Flying Contraptions, Ltd.
Box 17463
Nashville, TN 37127
(615) 834-7251

Free Flight of Greenville
c/o Formex Co.
100 Austin St.
Greenville, TN 37743

Wings of Greenville
Free Flight of Greenville
Box 254
Greenville, TN 37743

Butterfly, Inc.
1911 W. Cumberland
Knoxville, TN 37916

Raymond Garner
4431 Namur Grove
Memphis, TN 38109

Fly Cataloochee
Rt. 1, Box 500
Maggie Valley, NC 28751

Canada

Al Linkewich Hang Gliding School
Box 857, Red Deer
Edmonton, Alberta
Canada

Kartway Park Ltd.
9102-51 Ave.
Edmonton, Alberta
Canada

Big White Ski Development
RR 3, Hall Rd.
Kelowna, B.C.
Canada

Delta Wing Displays
Box 892
Kelowna, B.C.
Canada

Eagle Delta
Box 11
Invermere, B.C.
Canada
(604) 342-9415

Tod Mount Flying School
749 Victoria
Kamloops, B.C.
Canada

Bob Conners
5711 Blue Bell
W. Vancouver, B.C.
Canada

Kitslinno Marine Lumber Ltd.
1502 W. 2 Ave.
Vancouver, B.C.
Canada
(604) 736-0166

R. S. Woyma
20 Cloverdale Crescent
Winnipeg, Manitoba
Canada #2C 1Z1
(204) 222-2949

Mesle Canada Reg'g.
Box 610, RR 5
Ottawa, Ontario
Canada K1G 3N3

Free Flight of Midland
Midland Mike's Special Sports
Box 614
Midland, Ontario
Canada

Skysurfing Unlimited
621 Redwood Ave.
Ottawa, Ontario
Canada K2A 3E8

Asia, Australia, Europe, South America

Sky Craft Pty. Ltd.
138 Bellevue Parade, Suite 122
Carlton, NSW 2218
Australia

Ultra Light Flight Systems
c/o Steven Choen
15 Grand Parade
Brighton Le Sands
NSW 2216 Australia

Bill Moyes
173 Bronte Rd.
Waverly, Sydney
Australia

McBroom Sailwings Ltd.
12 Manor Court Dr.
Horfield Common
Bristol, England BS7 OXF

Hi Kites
c/o David Walling
20 Aldsworth Close
Fairford GLSO
England GL7 41B

Critchley-Hughes Co.
c/o Edmond Critchley
8 Oak Tree Close
Virginia Water, Surrey,
England

Champfort-Sports
c/o Mike Wyer
Rte. de Mont d Arbvis
74120 Megeve
France

Aquilone Delta
Corvara' Badia
Italy

Delta Glider
7021 Stetten' Filder
Bernhauser STR 31
West Germany

Pacific Kites Ltd.
Box 45-087
Te Atatu
Aukland, New Zealand

New Zealand Gliding Kiwi
Box 545
Tauranga, New Zealand

Swiss Delta
7550 Schuls
Switzerland

Chandelle Europa A.G.
c/o Roger Staub
Post Fach 26
8640 Rapperswil
Switzerland

Manta of Europe
Box 105
8058 Zurich Airport
Switzerland

Free Flight of Japan
4-2-3- Chuo
Nakanoku, Tokyo
Japan

Free Flight of Ecuador
Titan Cia Limited
10 De Agusto
608 of Castilla 3140
Quito, Ecuador

Books About Hang Gliding

Guide to Rogallo Flight, Basic, by Bob Skinner and Rich Finley, Illustrated, 30 pages. Can be ordered from Flight Realities, 1945 Adams Avenue, San Diego, CA 92116.

Hang Flight. A 64-page, step-by-step flight instruction manual for beginning and intermediate pilots. Includes 100 illustrations. Can be ordered from Eco-Nautics, Box 1154, Redlands, CA 92373.

Hang Gliding, The Basic Handbook of Skysurfing, by Dan Poynter. A 200-page overview of the activity, fully illustrated. Can be ordered from Dan Poynter, 2431 Calle Almonte, Santa Barbara, CA 93109.

Man-Powered Flight, by Keith Sherwin. Discusses the history, modern technology, and design considerations of human-powered flight. Can be ordered from USGHA, Inc., Box 66306, Los Angeles, CA 90066.

Simplified Performance Testing for Hang Gliders, by Jack Park. A 17-page booklet. Can be ordered from Jack Park, 15237 Lakeside, Sylmar, CA 91342.

Index

Acrobatics, 62, 98, 104
Aerobatics, 58, 99
Aerodynamics, 64, 65-66
  of Rogallo kite, 42, 44-48
Ailerons, 62
Airspeed indicators, 93, 113
Alcoholic beverages, 107
Altimeter, 62, 112, 113
Altitude, limit on, 136
Anemometer, 58
Annie Green Springs Hang Glider
    Championships, 107
Anodizing, 77
Approach control, 110–112
Assembling framework, 74-75

Bach, Richard, 36
Balance, learning, 86, 91, 91-92
Bamboo Butterfly, 27–29, 32, 37, 56,
    67, 115, 128
Bat Glider (hang glider), 17, 29

Batso (hang glider), 29, 32, 56, 58
Beetle (glider), 17
Bell, Alexander Graham, 24-25
Bennett, Bill, 36, 103, 105
Bicycle-pedal propellers, 119, 122-123
Bicycles, 10, 19, 50, 81, 119, 132
Big White Mountain Hang Glider
    Meet, 107
Biplane gliders, 30–34, 55, 56, 62, 67
Bird Flight as the Basis of Aviation
    (Lilienthal), 15
Bladud legend, 7
Blueprints, 73
Boat sails, 66, 76
Body shifting, 113–114, 116
Boenish, Carol, 105
Bonomi, Vittorio, 121
Borelli, G. A., 8
Bossi, Enea, 121
Bracing wires, 74
  preflight checks of, 84

Index

Brock, Hall, 76
Building gliders, 67–81
  assembling framework, 74–75
  attaching sail, 75–77
  cost of, 4, 67, 70, 77
  kits for, 67–68, 70, 73, 77–78
  maintenance, 79–80
  from plans, 67, 70–74
Bumper stickers, 3
Bungee launchers, 118

California Institute of Technology, 32,
    57
Carmichael, Bruce, 86
Cayley, Sir George, 10–13, 17
Championship competitions, 107–109
  See also names of meets
Chanute, Octave, 4, 18, 22, 30, 67
Chanute Hang Gliding Meet, 107
Childs, John, 8
Clarkson, Mark, 60–62, 85, 112, 113,
    135
Cliff launching, 95–97, 112
Clubs, 1, 131, 145–148
  See also names of clubs
Cole, Curtis, 36
Colver, Frank, 64, 65
Compasses, 113
Compressed air, 117
Conduit Condor (hang glider), 29
Conical Rogallo kite, 47
Control bar, 36, 45, 46, 47, 50, 87,
    89–91, 95, 100, 104, 136
  preflight check, 84
Control surfaces, 50, 52, 65
Control zones, 112
Cost:
  of building gliders, 4, 67, 70, 77
  of Rogallo kites, 37, 48, 67
Cronk, Dave, 52, 61, 64
Cronk 5 (glider), 64
Cronk Kite (glider), 52, 64, 66
Cronk Sail (glider), 64
Cross-country flying, 112, 113
Culver, Irv, 62
Cumulus clouds, 98
Cylindrical Rogallo kite, 49

Daedalus legend, 6–7, 8, 120
Damian, John, 8
Dante, 8
"Darius Green and His Flying
    Machine" (Trowbridge), 18–19
De Havilland Aircraft Company, 122
Dealers, 70, 155–174
Death Valley National Park, 2
Delta Kite Championships, 101
De Motum Animalium (Borelli), 8
Diamond Badges, 112, 116
Dirigibles, 9
Diurnal winds, 112
Drag racing, 39, 51
Dune buggies, 118

Eagles, 91
Eco-flight, 5, 24, 36–39, 48, 113
Ecosports, 119
Eipper, Dick, 60
Electronic equipment, 109
Elevator, 62
Encyclopaedia Britannica, 12–13
Endurance records, 94, 101, 106, 107,
    112–113
Experimental Aircraft Association,
    The, 69, 74–75

Fatalities:
  cause of, 50–51
  first airplane, 25
  in hang gliding, 4, 136
Faust, Joe, 37, 129–130, 133–134
Federal Aviation Administration
    (FAA), 34, 53, 71–72, 74, 112,
    132, 133–134, 136, 137
Figure eights, 95, 110
Finnery, Zeke, 105
Flaps, 50
Flare, of wings, 51, 93
"Fleep" (Flying Jeep), 43
"Flex-Wing" craft, 43
Flight instruments, 50, 61–62, 82,
    109, 112–113, 117
  See also names of instruments
Flying, 82–99
  getting airborne, 91–94
  instruction in, 86–91

preflight checks, 84–86
ridge soaring, 95–97
riding the wind, 94–95
sites for, 83–84, 85, 95
thermal soaring, 58, 60, 62, 95, 97–99, 101, 112, 126–127
Flying Trapeze, 88–89
Flying suits, heated, 118
Framework:
assembling, 74–75
attaching sail to, 75–77
Franco-Prussian War, 14
Fuselage, enclosed, 116, 117

Gardia, Ed, 136
Glider, first successful human flight in, 11–12
Gold Badges, 110
Ground crews, 87
"Ground Skimmer" (publication), 105, 131, 136, 148
Guide to Rogallo Flight—Basic, 108
Gull (glider), 17
Gusty winds, 92, 110

Haessler, Helmut, 121
Hand controls, 62
Hang Badge requirements, 110–112, 141–144
Hang Glider Manufacturer's Association (HMA), 69–70
Hang Glider Weekly (publication), 128, 146
Hang Gliding:
beginnings of, 6–19
building gliders, 67–81
decline of, 19–22
flying, 82–99
toward human-powered planes, 5, 115–128
popularity of, 1–5, 129–138
rebirth of, 23–39
rigid wing gliders, 51, 54–66, 79, 80
Rogallo kites, 2, 3–4, 24–32, 34–35, 37, 40–53, 76, 94, 100, 103, 105–108, 112, 115, 118, 134, 135, 137

soaring, 5, 13, 21–22, 23, 40, 55, 60, 62, 83, 94–99, 100–114, 132, 133
Hang Gliding Park, 101, 137
Hang Loose (biplane glider), 4, 30–31, 32, 37, 54, 64, 67, 70, 117
Hang soaring, *see* Soaring
Harness, 47, 87, 88, 89, 95
preflight checks of, 84–86
Hatfield Club, 122
Hawk (glider), 17, 18
Hawks, 91
Heated flying suits, 118
Helicopters, 8
Horizontal axis, 45, 46
Hot-air balloon, 2–3, 9–10, 13
Hughes, John, 106
Human-powered airplane, 5, 115–128
historical background of, 120
Kremer award for, 121–124
in the 1930s, 120–121
with pedals, 118–120, 122, 126, 128
ultralight sailplanes, 114, 115–118, 119, 133

Icarus (hang gliders), 1, 55–59, 60, 64, 117
Icarus I (biplane glider), 32, 56
Icarus II (biplane glider), 34, 57–58, 60, 98
Icarus III (glider), 58
Icarus IV (glider), 58
Icarus V (glider), 34, 56, 58–59, 66, 73, 98, 117
Icarus legend, 6–7, 120
Instruction, 86–88
Instruments, 50, 61–62, 82, 109, 112–113, 117
See also names of instruments
Internal Revenue Service, 27

Jensen, Volmer, 24, 31, 53, 62–64, 73, 136
Jobe, Jeff, 36, 103–104
Jonathan Livingston Seagull (Bach), 36
Jupiter (pedal craft), 124

Keel, 74
  preflight checks, 84
Kiceniuk, Taras, Sr., 29, 32, 110
Kiceniuk, Taras, Jr., 29, 32-34, 53,
  56-59, 62, 64, 98, 117
Kilbourne, Dave, 2, 34-35, 103
Kilbourne, Rich, 39
King posts, preflight check of, 84
Kishazy, Rudy, 105-106
Kite skiing, 101-104
Kites, 10, 11
  Chinese, 10, 24
  See also Rogallo kites
Kits, glider, 67-68, 70, 73
  buying, 77-78
Kitty Hawk Hang Glider Day, 107
Kiwi birds, 91
Kocsis, Chuck, 137
Kocsis Fund, 137
Koman, Mike, 68
Kremer, Henry, 121-122, 123
Kremer Prize, 121-128

Labatts Brewery, 107
Lambie, Jack, 30, 37, 54, 67, 70, 117-
  118
Lambie, Mark, 30-31
Landing gear, 50, 91
Landing wheel, 116, 121
  pedal drive for, 118-120
Landings:
  learning, 91-94
  techniques, 88, 89
  into the wind, 95-97
Larson, Mike, 108
Lasham Gliding Centre, 122
Lateral axis, 46
Lateral control, 88
Launching from a cliff, 95, 112
Leading edges, 74
  preflight checks, 84
Lectures, for instruction, 86
Levitation, 130
Libelle (sailplane), 116
Licher, Lloyd, 28
"Lifestyle!" (publication), 36
Lift, 51, 60, 113
Lilienthal, Otto, 3, 4, 14-17, 20, 22,
  107, 130

Lilienthal Memorial Hang Gliding
  Championships, 4, 58, 62, 69,
  107, 138
Linnets (pedal craft), 124
Lippish, Alexander, 120, 125
Longitudinal axis, 45, 46
Lovejoy, Bob, 53, 60
Low, Slow and Out of Control
  (newsletter), 129-130, 133-134
Luffing, 66

MacCready, Paul, 28
McMasters, John, 36, 50, 124-125
Maintenance, 79-80
Maintenance and Repair (Soaring
  Society of America), 75
Malliga (pedal craft), 124
Man-powered Aircraft Group (Royal
  Aeronautical Society), 121
Man-Powered Flight (Sherwin), 125
Manufacturers, 68-69, 77, 131, 149-
  154
Markowski, Mike, 45
Massachusetts Institute of Technology
  (MIT), 125
Matros, Rich, 105
Mayfly (pedal craft), 123
Midnight Flyer,, 56
Miller, Richard, 27-29, 37, 56, 65, 67,
  86, 94, 115-116, 119, 129, 132,
  137
Model airplanes, 10-11, 44, 74
  first flying, 11
Monoplane gliders, 58, 62, 65
Montgomery, John J., 3, 4, 13-14, 24,
  107, 109
Montgomery Glider Flight Com-
  petition, 3, 107-109
Motorboats, kites towed by, 34-35
Motorcycles, 3, 138
Movable controls, 114
Movies, for instruction, 86
Moyes, Bill, 36, 103
MPA-1 (pedal craft), 124
Mt. Palomar Obseratory, 32
Mufli (pedal craft), 121

Napoleon I (emperor), 10

National Aeronautics and Space
Administration (NASA), 23,
24, 25, 26-27, 42, 43
National Hang Gliding Cham-
pionships, 108
National Soaring and Hang Gliding
Festival, 107
Northrop Institute of Technology,
117, 125
Nosewheel, 84

Oliver of Malmesbury, 7
Olson, Jack, 118
Organizations, 1, 129-138, 145-148
  beginnings of USHGA, 130-131
  differences between, 132-136
  founding of Self-Soar Association,
  129-130
  and safety regulations, 136-137
  setting up flying sites, 137
  See also names of organizations
Ornithopter, 120
Overcontrolling, 91
Overweight pilots, 85-86

Palmers, Barry, 86
Parachutes, 8, 13, 25, 34, 40, 41, 42,
  43-44, 48, 50, 54, 74, 99
"Parasev" (flying kite), 43
Payne, Art, 23
Pedal drive, 118-120, 122, 126, 128
Pedaliante (pedal craft), 121
Peninsula Hang Glider Club, 130
Performance, of rigid-wing gliders,
  54-56, 58
Piggott, Derek, 122
Pilcher, Percy, 17-18, 22
Piper Cubs, 2-3, 103
Pitch, on lateral axis, 45, 46
Plans, building from, 67, 70-74
Popular Mechanics (publication), 67
Portability, of Rogallo kites, 48-50, 81
Potter, Lieutenant John, 124
Preflight checks, 84-86
Price, Chris, 105
Prone flying, 47
Public relations, 138
Publications, 1, 131, 148-149
  See also names of publications

Puffin (pedal craft), 120, 125
Pusher-type kite, 119

Quicksilver (glider), 60-62, 64, 66,
  113
Quicksilver B (glider), 70

Radios, 118
Raleigh, Sir Walter Alexander, 6
Ready-built gliders, 78-79
Reflex, in flying, 111
Regent Street Polytechnic School, 10
Rental flights, 99
Ridge soaring, 95-97
Rights of way, 111
Rigid-wing gliders, 51, 54-66, 79, 80
  building, 73
  cruising speed, 112
  Jensen designs for, 62-64
  Kiceniuk lead in, 56-59
  performance of, 54-56, 58
  Quicksilver, 60-62, 64, 113
  sailwing, 64-66
Roadtable airplane, 64
Rogallo, Francis M., 25-27, 41, 44,
  129
Rogallo, Gertrude Sugden, 25, 41
Rogallo airplane, 27
Rogallo Hang Glider Meet, 107
Rogallo kites, 2, 3-4, 24-32, 34-35,
  40-53, 76, 94, 100, 103-108,
  112, 115, 118, 134, 135, 137
  aerodynamics of, 42, 44-48
  basic components of, 47-48
  compared with rigid-wing gliders,
  54-56, 58-66
  cost of, 37, 48, 67
  development of, 24-27, 40-44
  good points, 48-51
  homebuilt, 69, 71, 73, 74
  improvements on, 52-53
  inflatable, 42
  maintenance, 80
  problems, 51-52
  ready-made, 79
  transporting, 48-50, 81
Roll, on longitudinal axis, 45, 46
Rotars, 111
Rowley, Karen, 5

Royal Aeronautical Society, 121, 124
Rudders, 58, 62
Ryan Aeronautical Company, 27, 43

"S" turns, 110, 111
Safety, 4, 50, 51, 64, 70, 132–133,
    134, 136–137, 138
Sail, attaching to frame, 75–77
Sailboats, 44, 45, 48, 49, 56, 74
Sailing, 39, 40
Sailplanes, 4, 21, 27, 35, 40, 48, 51,
    55, 56, 60, 61, 62, 63, 95, 98–
    99, 110, 111, 112, 113, 114,
    132, 134
  preflight checks, 84
  solar-powered, 127–128
  ultralight, 114, 115–118, 119, 133
Sailwing (glider), 64, 65
Sailwing design, 64–66
San Francisco Bay Bridge, 103
Sato-Maeda design (pedal craft), 124
Schools, 155–174
Schweizer 2–33 sailplane, 21, 56, 98
Seat harness, 47, 87–88, 95
Self-launched hang gliders, 117, 118,
    119
Selfridge, Lieutenant Thomas, 25
Self-Soar Association, 37, 129, 130
Sewing sails, 77
Shakespeare, William, 18
Sherwin, Keith, 125
Shock cords, 118, 120
Silver Badges, 111–114
Sink rate, 53, 56, 58
  of ultralight sailplane, 115, 116, 119
Sites, for flying, 83–84, 137
  preflight checks of, 85
  wind at, 94
Ski kites, 34
Skiing, 30, 36, 39, 44, 81, 84, 101,
    103–104
Sky surfing, 30, 46, 83, 85, 86
Skydiving, 50
Skysailing, *see* Hang gliding
Skysurfer Kite (glider), 45
Slatting, 66
Slope winds, 92, 97, 126
Smirnoff Sailplane Derby, 107

Smokey-the-Bear expeditions, 2, 105–
    106
SOAR (Save Our Airspace Resources),
    137
Soaring, 4, 13, 21–22, 23, 40, 55, 60,
    62, 83, 94–99, 100–114, 132,
    133
  championships, 107–109
  Hang Badge requirements, 110–
    111, 141
  ridge, 95–97
  Smokey-the-Bear trips, 2, 105–106
  stunt flying, 100–104, 106, 136
  thermal, 4, 58, 60, 62, 95, 98–99,
    101, 103, 110, 126–127
  winning Silver Badges, 111–114
Soaring (magazine), 27, 100, 117, 126,
    132, 133
Soaring Handbook (SSA), 133
Soaring Society of America (SSA), 75,
    112, 131, 132–136
Solar-powered sailplane, 127–128
So-Lo (glider), 62
Southampton University, 121
Southampton University Man-
    powered Air Craft (SUMPAC),
    121
Southern California Hang Gliding
    Association (SCHGA), 130, 132
Speedboats, kites towed by, 34–35
"Spoilers," 50
Spot landing, 101, 107, 110
Spray-painting, 77
Stability, 51, 65, 112
Stalls, 50, 91, 93–94, 95, 111–112
"Star Trek" spaceship, 63
Statue of Liberty, 103
Stunt flyers, 100–104, 106, 136
Supersoarers, 5, 113
Suppliers, 70
Surfing, 2, 29, 30, 47, 138
Swing seat, 36, 46, 58, 87
Swingwing (glider), 62–64, 73
Sylvester, Rick, 105

Tail assemblies, 118
Tail outrigger, 65
Takeoff, learning, 91–94
Technical Board (SSA), 133

Television, 79
Terminal velocity, 50
Thermal soaring, 4, 58, 60, 62, 95, 99,
    101, 103, 112, 126–127
Thistledown (flying wing), 115–117,
    119
360-degree turns, 97, 111
Toucan (pedal craft), 124
Transporting gliders, 48–50, 80–81
Trapeze control bar, 36, 45, 46, 47,
    50, 87, 88–89, 100, 136
Trowbridge, John Townsend, 18–19
Turn, on vertical axis, 45, 46
Turnbuckles, 71
Two-seat trainer, 86, 87

Ultralight Committee (SSA), 133
Ultralight sailplanes, 114, 115–118,
    119, 133
Ultralite Products, 69
U.S. Army, 25, 43
United States Hang Gliding
    Association (USHGA), 101,
    105, 137
  beginning of, 130–131
  Hang Badge requirements, 110–
    111, 141–145
United States Hang Gliding Cham-
    pionships, 107
University of California at Los Angeles
    (UCLA), 130
Ursinus, Oskar, 121

Variometer, 62, 112, 113
Vertical axis, 45, 46

Villinger, Franz, 121
Vinci, Leonardo da, 6, 8, 11, 41, 120
Volkswagen, 81

Water skiing, 34, 41, 46, 101–103, 104
Waterman, Waldo, 64
Waterman-Seagull Flyer (glider), 64
Weight watching, 85–86
Welding, 77
Weybridge MPA (pedal craft), 123
"Whisper of the Butterfly" (Payne), 23
Wills, Bob, 101, 106, 136
Wills, Chris, 136
Wills, Eric, 136
Wills brothers, 100
Wills wing gliders, 106
Wimpenny, John, 122, 124
Wind, landing into, 95–97
Wind meters, 58, 94
Wing assemblies, 118
Wing struts, 58
Woodford machine, 123
World Professional Hang Gliding
    Championships, 107
World War I, 20, 120
World War II, 23, 121
Wortmann, Dr. F. X., 65–66
Wright brothers, 1, 4, 13, 19–20, 22,
    23, 25, 27, 30, 82, 97, 107, 109,
    120
  first powered flight of, 19–20

X-15 rocket plane, 24

Yaw, on vertical axis, 45, 46
Yosemite National Park, 2, 105